Pioneering
Moral Education

Pioneering Moral Education

VICTOR COOK AND HIS FOUNDATION

W. A. Gatherer

EDINBURGH UNIVERSITY PRESS

Frontispiece: Victor Cook. By courtesy of the *Press and Journal*, Aberdeen.
Extract on pp. 82–40: by courtesy of the *Press and Journal*, Aberdeen.
Extract on p. 89: by courtesy of the *Times Educational Supplement Scotland*.
Extract on pp. 103–6: *The Courier*, Dundee © D. C. Thomson & Co., Ltd.

© W. A. Gatherer, 2004

Edinburgh University Press Ltd
22 George Square, Edinburgh

Typeset in Minion by
Pioneer Associates, Perthshire, and
printed and bound in Great Britain by
The Cromwell Press, Trowbridge, Wilts

A CIP record for this book is available from the British Library

ISBN 0 7486 2118 0 (hardback)

Contents

Acknowledgements

Thanks to my fellow trustees of the Gordon Cook Foundation, who asked me to write this book and have been supportive and patient during its parturition; a special thank you to Gavin Ross for his advice and assistance; a very special thank you to Irene Brown, without whose cheerful encouragement, skill and hard work the book could never have been made.

Foreword

As the most recently appointed Trustee of the Gordon Cook Foundation in 2001 I never knew Victor Cook; indeed, although involved for twenty-five years in education I must confess I was not aware of his Foundation. Furthermore I have no professional experience in primary or secondary schools. It was therefore with considerable humility that I agreed to write this Foreword, notwithstanding the fact that such a task almost inevitably falls on me due to my current occupation of the chair of trustees.

Yet I am pleased to do so for one important reason: Bill Gatherer has written an evocative and engrossing account of an extraordinary man and his passion; in so doing he has served well the interests of the Foundation and the memory of Victor Cook, and it gives me great pleasure to record here the gratitude of his fellow trustees for his endeavours. You, the reader, have a treat in store. Through the pages of this book I feel I almost knew Victor. Certainly in articulating this inspiring tale of one man's driving beliefs and commitment, Bill enables one to empathise with Victor Cook's objects and admire his dedication and energy in seeking to bring his beliefs to fruition. Bill knew Victor well and was a founder trustee. This account is both personal and professional and it is from this basis, along with Bill's scholarship and wide experience in education, that the book is such a joy to read.

The objects of the Foundation relating to Citizenship Education and Character Development as stated in its Deed of Trust are clear in their purposes, yet drafted in such a way as to enable the trustees to exercise their judgement and discretion as to how they may be achieved within the ever-changing circumstances of society. Whilst embracing timeless values that have guided mankind throughout the ages we as trustees can freely consider the challenges of contemporary moral education. It is my belief that the latitude given to us in interpreting the Foundation's objects has enabled us to maintain a freshness of purpose that invigorates our involvement in its work.

This book makes clear Victor Cook's lifelong determination that a realisation of the moral values that guide society towards its general wellbeing can be achieved through a process of education. The Gordon Cook Foundation, through its trustees, is determined to interpret the objects of the Deed of Trust in a manner most appropriate to the conditions that prevail within society and to initiate educational approaches towards the attainment of the values espoused by the Deed of Trust. This book will certainly serve to encourage and inform our efforts, and also, I feel sure, will stimulate a wide readership to understand and consider the important issues in modern moral education. At the risk of appearing presumptuous I am sure that, modest man though he was, Victor Cook would be pleased with this book.

GAVIN ROSS

To the memory
of
Maimie Gatherer

Chapter One

The life and times of Victor Cook

The world Victor Cook was born into, in 1897, was politically dominated by problems of Empire: Britain ruled a quarter of the world's population spread over almost a quarter of its area, and was constantly struggling to maintain its imperial discipline in a gigantic, multi-racial, polyglot and restless conglomeration of dependencies. Apart from the recently autonomous dominions of Canada, Australia and New Zealand, all politically modelled on the mother country and anxious to preserve and develop her traditions and values, the Empire was under the subjection of an authoritarian, if largely benign, government in London. A large administrative structure of agencies and departments linked to London ministries attempted to rule the lives of the subject peoples according to a model which was varied to suit regional and local needs only so far as it was thought necessary for the maintenance of peace and economic progress. The colonial civil services were staffed by men from British middle-class homes, well educated and strongly motivated to carry out their duties – represented often as 'the white man's burden' – with honesty, industry and loyalty. (Women did not figure much among the rules: the few heroic nuns and missionaries dedicated to teaching and medicine were much admired but not officially empowered.)

The Scottish society in which Victor grew up was strongly representative of the people who ruled the Empire. His forebears were farmers, innkeepers, shrewd businessmen assiduously seeking wealth by working hard and saving and buying into small thriving enterprises such as horse transport and yeoman farming. Victor's grandfather was all of these: farmer, innkeeper, proprietor of a coaching firm, and a clever speculator. In 1889, having settled in Aberdeen, he bought an iron foundry and began to develop the company of Barry, Henry and Cook which became the main focus of Victor's life. His grandfather was more than a clever and energetic businessman: he was a director of several other companies and he entered regional politics as a county councillor. Victor's father Robert was the youngest of four sons, all of whom followed traditional middle-class Victorian careers – marine engineering, overseas posts, banking, farming. Robert worked in the family business and helped it to prosper

1

during the Edwardian and First World War years. He married Victoria Gordon, daughter of a wealthy Deeside farmer and businessman; he had some pretensions to local grandeur and was often invited to Balmoral Castle. Victor's name enshrined a family tradition: he was named after his grandfather, his father and his mother ('Victor' to betoken 'Victoria'). His schooling was also middle-class traditional: he attended Aberdeen's most prestigious private school, now Robert Gordon's College, before studying to prepare himself for a career in engineering at Glasgow University and then the Royal Technical College, famed for its practical engineering courses. Just prior to his father's death he entered the family business (giving up a promising contract with the Island Trading Company of Borneo); and by 1923, at the age of 26, he was Chairman and Managing Director of the company, with his mother and his brother Norman as major shareholders. Norman added a share in a motor car business to the family's enterprises; but when he died as a result of a motor cycle accident in 1927, Victor was left alone, with his mother, to run the firm. They lived together in a suburban mansion, Countesswells House, from 1931 until his mother died in 1965; thereafter Victor lived alone, with a housekeeper and gardener and occasional extra helpers, until his death in 1990. He never married. His mother, by all accounts an energetic and somewhat imperious woman, was the central figure in his social milieu for most of his life. By the beginning of the 1970s he had managed a big engineering business, through good times and bad, for half a century; and in 1973, as sole owner, he sold a controlling interest to a company dealing among other things in North Sea Oil off-shore services.

The code of values that predominated in the Scotland where Victor grew up and developed his career derived mainly from the Christian ethic preached by highly educated ministers of the Kirk of Scotland. Obedience to Christian moral doctrines and devotion to the Crown were central tenets. Patriotism and loyalty to one's lawful superiors motivated alike the empire builders and the public servants at home. Charity was also an important aspiration. Helping the poor to survive, improving their lot in life and educating them were genuine aims for the best of the more affluent in their progress towards Christian fulfilment. But they could see little point in attempting to change the mechanisms of power. They perceived poverty as a kind of universal condition, escapable only by individuals endowed with innate ability, willingness to work hard and the force of character that is so necessary a factor of success in life.

But these were important values. For generations Scots had clung to the faith that a 'lad o' pairts', a youth with brains and industry, could succeed in life whatever the circumstances of his birth. What was necessary was force of character, a good education and physical ability to make use of it. Social change was much to be desired: more and better hospitals, better nutrition for the poor, more and better schools and better means of access to higher education should all be provided by the community aided by personal charity. Social reform by means of political action, such as the forcible redistribution of wealth, was not envisaged, except by the small but growing groups of radicals – communists, democratic socialists, liberal reformers – which flourished in the large urban areas but not in the staid countryside or wealthy residential suburbs.

Education was the key, both to success in life and to the amelioration of social and economic conditions among the poor. Free schooling was already available to all, but the ideal that everyone should be able to fulfil whatever abilities and ambitions they possessed was a long way from being realised. It was starkly apparent that only a small percentage of young people were able to enter higher education. Real efforts were made to help abler children. In every Scottish parish local benefactors helped children to acquire the qualifications required; most grammar schools had bursary schemes to help less affluent parents keep their children on to the higher classes; every district in the north-east of Scotland benefited from bequests and endowments left by successful lads o' pairts such as James Dick and John Milne. The universities had bursary competitions from which the winners gained financial help. In the early years of the twentieth century the Carnegie Trust (endowed by the most successful of all lads o' pairts) met the class fees, or a substantial portion of them, of nearly every student in Scotland. It was still the case, however, that half or more of Scots children were unable to enter higher education until near the end of the century: poor living conditions and the demands of an excessively academic curriculum combined to inhibit the long-held aspirations which people like Victor Cook cherished.

The values underpinning these educational benefactions were power-fully reinforced by the so-called 'presbyterian work ethic' that had developed in Scotland throughout the centuries since the religious reformation of the 1560s. John Knox and his colleagues declared that, along with cleanliness, honesty and unselfishness, industriousness was a prime value to be taught in schools. Hard work was an integral compo-nent of 'good character', which along with Christian faith was the main objective of education. They held, moreover, that hard work brings legitimate material rewards. The parable of the talents was interpreted literally to generations of pupils. Profits from honest labour were hallmarks of hard work and shrewd business. As a great Victorian lad o' pairts, Thomas Carlyle, put it, 'There is a perennial wholeness and even sacredness in Work . . . in idleness alone is there perpetual despair.'

Victor Cook was strongly representative of the Scots middle-class in his own times. He never doubted the need to live a Christian life, though he was not a devout member of the kirk. He was patriotic, but not uncritically. He believed in the virtues of hard work and fair dealing, while he exercised all the shrewdness required for success in a competitive trade; he was known to be 'a good boss', honest and insistent on requiring scrupulous honesty from his staff. He subscribed to the prevailing belief in the need for self-improvement through hard work and studies. At the same time he believed firmly in the need to serve the community: what was known as 'civic virtue' by the eighteenth century Scots philosophers was heartily, if modestly, lived out in Victor's own life. He gave support to movements like the Boy Scouts, Boys' Brigade and Girl Guides; he gave financial support to local youth clubs and various good causes promoted by the church. In his private life he worked hard by reading and studying to improve his own understanding of the world, and above all of how it could be made a better place for the young to grow up in; his large and growing library testified to his enthusiasm for education. To Victor, as to many of his compatriots, education was the way forward, not only for the individual but also for society: accepting that human beings have a prime responsibility towards one another, he became eager to use his own wealth to help others to prosper, especially to prosper in their human sympathies and their ability to live decent, honest and useful lives.

Chapter Two

Towards the Foundation

Victor Cook was always an assiduous reader and buyer of books. We can gather from his library and writings that even while deeply involved in business he was keenly interested in the two major preoccupations of his life, education and health. He would occasionally tell friends that he would have liked to be a teacher of some kind, but he was compelled by circumstances to go into the family business. We know that circumstances did compel him to return to Aberdeen to join the firm, but if his father's illness had not intervened it is likely that he would have pursued a career in engineering and business abroad. At any rate his interest in education and especially in teaching was clearly evident to all who knew him in later life. His emergence as an advocate of specialised moral education in the sixties cannot have been sudden; there was certainly a considerable amount of reading and reflection behind it.

We know that he was able to take an active interest in health education in the 1940s. In 1949 he purchased the whole of the library of the New Health Society – more than a thousand volumes. The society was formed in the 1920s by a surgeon of Guy's Hospital, Sir Arbuthnot Lane, and it was dedicated to the promotion of education in nutrition, health education and alternative and preventative medicine. Victor offered the collection, along with an oil painting of Lane, to Aberdeen City Library, but asked that it be housed in Countesswells House during his lifetime. He was, over the next four decades, regularly consulting the works. He was firmly convinced that health education should feature prominently in schools and further education institutions; in the documentation related to the Foundation he stipulated that health education should be a major objective, second only to character education.

In his personal life he was much concerned with questions of nutrition: what foods best led to physical fitness, how foods should be kept free of pollutants, what were the secrets of healthy living and survival. He bought books which might fairly be called popular guides to healthy eating, and he would enthuse to his friends about the wisdom of any recent acquisition. One of these was Doris Grant's book, *Your Daily Food, Recipe for Survival*, published in 1973 by Faber and Faber. Mrs Grant had long been writing and agitating about the dangers of modern processed foods to both physical and mental wellbeing, focussing attention particularly on refined carbohydrates – white flour and white sugar – and the low fibre diet they led people to follow. She predicted that the deterioration of the nation's food would result in a serious deterioration of the nation's health. She pointed to the prevalence in foodstuffs of toxic and carcinogenic substances such as nitrates, cyclamates, synthetic dyes, flour bleaches and a long list of other chemical additives; and she urged her readers to change their dietary habits in favour of high fibre foods such as bran, whole wheat and vegetables. She recommended honey as a substitute for sugar. She insisted we should shun cola drinks, commercial ice-cream, tinned meats, potato crisps, peanut butter and other foods containing preserving antioxidants; and she preached the virtues of fresh vegetables, unprocessed cheese, salads and fresh fruit. Governments, she said, should enforce the listing of all ingredients on labels, disclosing the names of all the additives; and obviously we should all be taught what these implied for our health. She quoted an extract from the *Washington Post*:

H. Herbert Fox tells me that the other night he ate some delicious citric acid mixed with propylene glycol, assorted glycerines, butylated hydroxyanisole, butylated hydroxytoluene and propyl gallate. Until he read the full list of ingredients on the package, Herb had been under the impression that he had just been munching on some tasty corn chips.

Victor shared Mrs Grant's convictions and admired her courageous reforming zeal; like her, he was himself a missionary for new attitudes towards everyday features of life. He was not skilled at expounding his enthusiasms. When he brought a copy of *Your Daily Food* to our house to present to my wife, proclaiming its message, he sounded like a food faddist and crank; when we read it we realised how important its arguments were: it was a message that thirty years later is being taught vigorously – if to some extent in vain – in the schools, newspapers, television and radio, and it has won the status of an educational priority.

The governing interest in Victor's life was, of course, education. We can only guess what his views were before he launched his personal campaign, during the sixties, to establish moral education and citizenship in the curriculum. Before then, certainly, he was reading about history, civilisation and culture in a wide variety of generalist books by popularisers like Arthur Bryant, Arnold Toynbee and William Barclay, a Scots Presbyterian minister. He was reading about education in official reports, in pamphlets issued by the World Education Fellowship and other societies, and he was reading the *Daily Telegraph* and other ephemera. Clearly, in the early years of the decade, he was forming ideas about moral education and the need for its being taught in schools, and the death of his mother in 1965 gave him time and motivation to pursue these interests. It was, he later recorded, a 'conversation' with Lord Reith that stimulated him especially: Reith suggested that he should submit his proposals in writing and formulate 'a practical, flexible Scheme of suggestions for use in schools'. This was in 1966.

The following year, in February, Victor called on Alexander Young, Director of Education for Aberdeen County, 'to ascertain whether he approved generally, without commitment to detail, a scheme which included proposals for explicit moral teaching in schools'. Victor told the director that he had promised to send to Lord Reith a 'memorandum' on the subject and wanted Mr Young's 'observations and approval' before doing so. According to a report issued by the county education committee in 1970, the interview 'set Mr Young thinking about moral education' and in due course a Moral Education Committee was set up. Victor was invited to join it but left after a few months, no doubt because he felt frustrated by the cautiousness of the approach the others were advocating, and there can be little doubt that they found his passionate convictions hard to put up with.

John Marshall, one of Victor's oldest friends and a valued adviser, recalls that 'a few years before the actual establishment of the Foundation Mr Cook had gathered a little group of well-wishers whom he called together at very rare intervals to discuss the "business" aspects of his projects'. But he seems to have found little reassurance about 'explicit' moral teaching. In Reith's agreement that something must be done about 'some of the troubles that were affecting the young people today' Victor could hope for important support. Reith was the first and most famous Director General of the BBC; he had retired from that post in 1938 but had remained in the public eye as a Member of Parliament, a government minister during the war, a writer and broadcaster. In 1948 the BBC initiated a series of lectures named the Reith Lectures after their 'founder', and this added to his fame. Victor's personal acquaintanceship with Reith occurred in the last five years of the great man's life; by then he was ageing, very deaf, but still vigorous and pleased to advise this rich but diffident Scots businessman eager to invest heavily in moral educational enterprises. Reith and Cook seemed to agree that young people were growing up 'with wrong attitudes of mind' and they could be brought up to live decent lives as good citizens. Both seemed to agree that the old 'abiding verities' and 'traditional virtues' were being abandoned.

But there were salient differences in the characters and outlook of the two men. Reith was proud, assertive and opinionated, while Cook was modest, quiet mannered and tentative in expressing his opinions, strongly felt as they might be. It was characteristic of Victor that he sought constantly for approval and reassurance from people who had achieved some eminence in the professions, particularly in medicine and education. Reith's endorsement of his proposals was of great importance to him. But the tenor of Victor's thought was markedly different from Reith's. The essential kindliness of his nature, combined with his apparent readiness to be guided by the professionals who advised him, led him to avoid the acerbic pessimism of Reith, with its apocalyptic vision of social degeneracy brought about by the hedonism of modern times and the prevailing indifference to Christian moral teachings. Victor's vision was limited, his mind dwelling on what better education could do for the young, so that they could develop 'maturity of character', self-discipline and 'concern for the wellbeing and happiness of others'. The positive, optimistic tendency of Victor's thinking contrasted strongly with the negative bleakness of conservative reactionaries like Reith. For Victor, the true objective of moral education was, as he said, 'to cultivate an affectionate, loving nature'. It was the great goal of his life to produce a systematic rationale and methodology that would enable schools to do that.

One of the most powerful sources of inspiration and learning for Victor at this time was William McDougall's book, *Character and the Conduct of Life*. McDougall was a leading psychologist in the early decades of the twentieth century, the major exponent of 'instinct theory', which posited that all human behaviour was activated by inherited or innate dispositions such as pugnacity, self-assertion, gregariousness and the desire to procreate, all related to bodily needs. Instincts were thought to motivate behaviour, but not consciously. Later theorists discounted McDougall's system on the grounds that it was circular: people tend to invent new instincts to explain new behavioural goals. In 1927 McDougall published his study of character and conduct, not as an academic psychologist but as what he described as a 'sophist', whose business was to help men to live wisely. The role of sophism, he said, 'is to aid some men and women to reflect profitably on the conduct of their own lives and to avoid some of the errors which, even though venial, may yet render them less happy than they might be or even go far to wreck their lives completely'. He wanted his book to take on the task of influencing others, more especially young people, to help them become better, happier, more successful.

This was precisely what Victor Cook wanted to do. And the premises which McDougall chose for his work matched the central beliefs on which Victor built his life's work. Two 'facts':

> first, that many men desire to live wisely and to live well, preferring good to evil; secondly, that in spite of the widely different answers returned by philosophers to their problems, men of all ages and of the most diverse creeds and civilisations are pretty well agreed as to what is good and what bad in conduct and character...

McDougall claimed that his long academic study of the 'raw material of human nature' qualified him to proffer practical guidance in the conduct of life. To a modern reader, the author's scientific experience does not seem to exempt him from ordinary prejudices and special pleading; but he does write, on the whole, with intelligence and insight, and his recurrent plea for reflective self-criticism has a modern resonance, especially for educators interested in personal and social education. His extended definitions of such terms as intelligence, sympathy, introspection and disposition would have been helpful to Victor: looking through Victor's copy of the book one can see many marked passages that appear in his own writings. But McDougall's long exposition of character and how it develops is essentially deterministic: to Victor, character development was a simple process of nourishing young, pliable minds by means of teaching; McDougall's continuing attempts to explain all behaviour in terms of instinctive dispositions was too subtle and complex for Victor.

Another important source of inspiration for Victor was E. B. Castle's *Moral Education in Christian Times*, published in 1958. Here, and later in Castle's book *The Teacher*, Victor was introduced to progressivist educational thinkers such as Pestalozzi and Froebel, with their message that good teaching, like good parenthood, is founded on love, on giving the child freedom to respond to good influences. Castle also points to the need for teachers to have defined structures for their teaching, to follow systematic processes and to relate everything they do to the needs of the children. Victor was strongly attracted to the concept of freedom, and also to the idea that freedom and discipline were complementary. Castle explained that freedom is a product of discipline, and that it was self-discipline that children need. He gave Victor an introduction to the

9

theories that underpin all good modern teaching. In his own writings, however, Victor evinced a lack of the language teachers use, tending to employ an old-fashioned style, spattered with capital letters and using weakly structured sentences; and his dependence on long extracts from his favourite mentors, most of them badly linked to the preceding and following propositions, added to the effect that teachers found his handbooks dull and irrelevant. All this unfortunately tended to conceal the important insights which Victor gained from his reading of McDougall and Castle. These authors had three main contributions to his thinking and the work he undertook. Firstly, they reinforced his belief that character development was not only highly desirable as an educational objective, but also that it was achievable, given the right conditions. Secondly, they encouraged him to believe that education for character cannot merely be left to the coincidental effects of the rest of schooling – it cannot merely 'rub off' from traditional teaching. Thirdly, they gave him new perspectives on education: the importance of the early years; the centrality of the home and the need for teacher-parent collaboration; the importance of 'flexibility' – that is, of designing learning and teaching in terms of actual pupils' needs and not only in keeping with prescribed injunctions. They also served to support advice he was receiving over the next few years, when he was trying to compile the details of his 'Plan'; for example, the need for research, professional reflection and experimentation, and above all the overriding importance of working with and under the guidance of practising teachers.

Chapter Three

Victor as lobbyist

The 'practical, flexible Scheme of suggestions for use in school' which Victor put together for Lord Reith's approval was seen by a number of people during 1967 and 1968, and one or two teachers agreed to 'test' the ideas in their classrooms. What he called 'First Tests' were held in Inverurie Academy (the rector, Dr Norman Dixon, was a member of the Moral Education Committee which Victor briefly sat on); and in Robert Gordon's College, where the headmaster, Jack Marshall, one of Victor's most helpful advisers, persuaded one of his staff to try out the materials. Since Victor spent the next twenty years revising, adding to and amending his subject matter, it is difficult to know precisely what the teachers were expected to do. The so-called 'Plan' consisted of a list of Objectives and Guiding Principles (capitals were important to him) along with a list of Topics intended to form the basis of a series of lessons. Like most lay persons interested in education, his understanding of the teaching and learning processes was simplistic. He was exclusively concerned with the content rather than the process of teaching, assuming that it was a matter of talking to the pupils, asking them questions about the subject matter and then getting them to write compositions about it. At that time he had little or no experience of visiting classrooms or talking with teachers and pupils.

In 1968 the Secretary of State for Scotland, Gordon Campbell, set up a committee to review current practices with regard to moral and religious education, and to make recommendations for its improvement. The chairman was W. Malcolm Millar, Professor of Mental Health in Aberdeen University. In the course of its work the committee conducted surveys among the major bodies concerned and invited anyone interested to submit their views on moral education. In the final report it emerged that no education authority made any specific recommendations or require-ments to their schools, and none had any person specially appointed to advise on or develop moral education: 'This does not, of course, mean that moral education is neglected, but only that it is usually regarded as a general aspect of the whole school work.' Several authorities had appointed working parties of teachers to examine this general area. On the question,

'How should moral education be developed in the future?' the evidence submitted was 'rather limited'. But the submission sent in by Victor Cook was treated with respect. Only a small group took the view that moral education could not be left to indirect teaching:

> but, as Mr Robert C. V. Cook puts it, 'would require the same systematic attention with definite periods based on research and experiment which other subjects already have.' Mr Cook submitted to the Committee a detailed plan for the character development of the child. This consisted of two stages. Stage One has the following sections: Introductory notes; Present practice; Theoretical considerations; Explicit moral education; Health notes; Applied ethics; Syllabuses; Teacher's section; Library code and class books. Stage Two comprises: Parents Committee; School and home; Youth association; Religious education. Mr Cook under his headings brings in all the elements that have to be considered in the development of moral education.

It is somewhat surprising that so much attention was paid to Victor's submission. His 'detailed plan' consisted only of the headings. Other submissions, for example by some humanist groups, were merely reported briefly. It seems likely that the chairman knew, or knew of, the locally prominent Mr Cook. It is also surprising that Victor does not seem ever to have referred much to his submission and its appearance in the text of this important report. This was possibly because he found the report's treatment of moral education disappointing. Some years later he referred to its 'tremendous vagueness'. It described an educational scene in which discussion of moral and social questions was virtually non-existent: in a large majority of the schools it was reported that such questions were raised and dealt with 'incidentally as the occasion arises'. Teaching specifically aimed at developing an understanding of moral issues – not in the context of religious education – not only seldom happened but was not considered to be a valid activity: as the Headmasters Association put it, 'Moral education without reference to religious belief would be an arid, depersonalised and ineffective exercise.' Strong representations from Church authorities insisted that 'the capacity of a school to develop moral and social values depends on its Christianity – not vice versa'. The Millar Committee concluded that it was the general point of view in Scotland that moral education should not at any stage be defined as a special subject or object of study; it was involved in nearly all subject teaching, in the attitudes and personalities of the staff, in the tone of the school, in its structure of authority and in putting examples before children of exemplary men and women. Despite this, the report devotes eight paragraphs to accounts by experts of the stages of development children go through towards moral maturity; Victor's great mentor William McDougall figured largely and his 'stages' were described in a manner reminiscent of Victor's own writings.

There was a great deal in the report that ought to have encouraged Victor in his endeavours, especially the evidence of a clamant need for more research and development work and the clear indications that, whatever the problems might be in the curricular implementation of it, there was a general acceptance that schools ought to accept responsibility for at least contributing to the moral education of their pupils. It was also apparent that many people, despite the majority of voices against or indifferent to his proposals, were at least open to further persuasion. If he had contacted the many bodies and individuals that evinced an interest he could have built up a network of allies. But by this time Victor had the bit between his teeth. He was determined to refine his Plan and have it implemented. He had also made up his mind that he would invest a considerable portion of his wealth in the campaign. He was also very keen to play a 'hands on' part in the design and application of school programmes.

Shortly after the 1970 election he wrote to the new Prime Minister, Edward Heath, describing his ideas and explaining that, being 'considerably in funds', he intended to set up a foundation to promote education for citizenship and character development, to which he himself would contribute to the extent of £100,000. Heath responded swiftly and approvingly. He sent a copy of the letter to Gordon Campbell, the Secretary of State for Scotland, and this was taken up by Hector Monro, the Scottish Minister for Education. Heath's initiative also put Victor in touch with appropriate civil servants in the Department for Education and Science (DES) and the Scottish Education Department (SED). In the meantime Victor was also receiving friendly, if eccentric, support from Lord Reith. The following letter was characteristic:

The Queen's House, Moray Place, Edinburgh 3
20 X 70

Dear Mr Cook
         Your letter of the 16th came here yesterday, and the one of 30.9.70 must have arrived here a week or more before we fetched up ourselves.

We have been enormously, and often infuriatingly, engaged on departure from London after 48 years, and then in trying to get things into shape here and they are unfortunately and most annoyingly far from that state.

The Gordon Cook Foundation document I have read carefully. What a task you have undertaken; I do indeed hope you will be successful to your own aspirations and standards.

Could we lunch at the New Club – but I am going right against my own principles and resolutions, because I have gotten more and more deaf, as a result of the crash I had over a year ago. I won't be a nuisance, deaf men are real nuisances, so I won't go among men, no social or gregarious associations at all and now I've suggested meeting you for lunch when you are in this city and free.

Yours very sincerely,
J. C. W. Reith

During the following years Victor was assiduously corresponding with a wide range of people likely to be interested in moral education. These included directors and officers of the Farmington Trust, which was set up in 1964 to study and promote education in religion and morality. Among the Council members were the Hon. E. R. H. Wills and Mr H. D. H. Wills, members of the wealthy tobacco family. In 1965 the Trust set up a Research Unit under the direction of John Wilson and based in Oxford. The main focus of the unit's work was moral education: 'to discover what conditions, contexts, types of teaching, etc. can best assist individuals to develop a coherent set of moral values within their societies, and to achieve the moral maturity to act on them.' As we shall see, Victor carefully studied the Articles of Association of the Farmington Trust and used them in drafting the deed of trust for his own Foundation. Correspondence and meetings with people of similar interest stimulated Victor to bring a group together to lobby the Schools Council, which had been set up in 1964 to advise the government on curriculum, teaching methods and examinations and to undertake projects of research and development. His new allies were John Blackie, a retired HM Inspector of Schools who had been responsible for primary education and who had written extensively on moral education; H. J. Scrogie, Staff Inspector of Religious Education in the Inner London Education Authority (ILEA); and Peter McPhail, director of the Moral Education Curriculum Project at Oxford. These highly respected experts agreed to be signatories to a Memorandum submitted to the Schools Council in June 1971. It was written by Victor in his easily recognisable style:

5th June, 1971

MEMORANDUM TO THE SCHOOLS COUNCIL

The four signatories of this Memorandum were brought together in the first instance by the initiative of one of them, Robert C. V. Cook, in order to discuss his proposals or any alternatives of a Standing Advisory Committee with functions forming an Information Centre on Moral Education, the essentials of which have been maintained in the final proposals. He was convinced of the importance of moral education, in its broadest sense, and had drawn up a carefully thought-out Scheme of explicit Moral Education intended, in the first instance, for use in Primary Schools. All the signatories share this conviction which is indeed very generally held. What is in doubt and what we feel needs systematic investigation, is how moral education is to be given. Traditionally, throughout the west, it has been part of religious instruction. Some of us are Christians and believe that moral education not based on the Christian faith lacks a dimension, but we all recognise that a substantial number of teachers and parents do not hold this faith, and we do not, in any case, consider that effective moral education is impossible without it.

We believe that moral education of some sort is made automatic by the mere fact of the human contacts and influences that operate in every school and home, and that if those influences are good the effects will correspond. Children learn the social virtues by belonging to communities in which they are practised. The importance of this implicit moral education is not in question, but we believe that children and young people need something explicit as well, that the making of choices, the consequences of actions and the balance of rights and duties need to be carefully considered and discussed.

We have, as individuals, initiated some small-scale experiments based on the above Scheme in schools in England and Scotland, designed to collect evidence for the view expressed above. This will take a little time. Meanwhile Mr Cook is taking steps to establish a Trust which will exist to encourage and support, in a variety of ways, the promotion of character training and health of mind and body. This Trust, to be known as the Gordon Cook Foundation, the terms of which have already been drawn up, will be established in the course of the next two to three years, and we consider that it will play a most valuable part in the support of promising and original experiments and development.

But we would suggest that one other thing is needed, that is, that a Project be established by the Schools Council to provide continuous support and information for teachers, utilising material developed both within and without the Council's work relating to the formation of character and good citizenship in the widest sense. The Project would follow up the work of the Moral Education Curriculum Project, Oxford, now nearing completion, of which one of our number is the Director, and would engage in the development and testing of curricular materials for Moral Education at the Primary and Middle Stages.

The Project would therefore have two functions:

(a) To provide an Information Centre including the after-care of related projects completed.
(b) Curriculum development at the Primary and Middle Stages.

Although the Project would have limited financial time, enquiries are meantime being made in an endeavour to maintain continuity on the termination of the Project with an Information Centre either at a College of Education or a Department of Education at a University.

The enquiries that have been set on foot regarding this work at certain schools in England and Scotland are limited and could not possibly deal with what is suggested above, being inadequate for providing the continuous material and information needed.

It is suggested that finance required might be considered at say £35,000 for a period of three years, including the services of a Director and Project Officer with the necessary professional staff.

As already stated, the Gordon Cook Foundation will not be formed until two to three years yet and could not deal with the above proposals, although the Trustees might well agree to finance particular projects and enquiries at the Committee's request. This matter is under consideration, and the outcome will partly depend on the Schools Council's response to our request.

Report after report, public utterance after public utterance, have emphasised the tremendous importance of giving to the rising generation a moral training which they can understand and respect and which will not appear to them to be ill-founded or unreasonable as they come to maturity. The Minister has promised top priority for Primary Education in the '70's and has expressed a hope for increasing emphasis on quality. We urge the Council to mount a project in which this promise is fulfilled and this hope encouraged.

The Schools Council reacted favourably, and in April 1972 the General Secretary, George Cooksey, wrote as follows to Victor:

SCHOOLS COUNCIL   160 Great Portland Street
                                              London W1N 6LL

                                                 28 April 1972

Dear Mr Cook,
        Now that the Moral Education Project for the Middle Years of Schooling has been approved by the Schools Council with Peter McPhail as Director, may I write to thank you for all your effort on behalf of this project, and to indicate how much the Council appreciates the work that you have already done in this field, which we trust will be of great value to the project itself.
        The Council is always pleased to see initiative such as yours relating to important curriculum development and I am sure that Mr McPhail would wish to associate himself with our thanks to you.

        With kind regards,
                            Yours sincerely,
                            G. W. Cooksey
                            Joint Secretary

R. C. V. Cook Esq.
Countesswells House
Bieldside
Aberdeenshire

The civil servants assigned to liaise with Victor as a result of Heath's initiative were W. J. H. Earl HMI and Eric Lord HMI from the Department for Education and Science, and W. K. Ferguson HMI from the Scottish Education Department. Between 1971 and 1975 there were several meetings and a spate of correspondence in which Victor pursued his own particular case for the furtherance of moral education. The official records of these meetings (if there were any) have not been preserved; but it was Victor's habit to take notes and to produce his own 'minutes' which he would then send to the others, and these have been kept among his papers. The first meeting seems to have been held on 5 December 1973, at the DES headquarters in Elizabeth House, London. According to Victor's minute, Mr Earl 'invited Mr Cook to report on his proposals to the Prime Minister in relation to the furtherance of Education for Citizenship considered in the widest sense.' Victor referred to his plea for the setting up of a National Consultative Council on Citizenship Education. If this were not considered 'suitable' he would hope that, in Scotland, there might be set up a Central Committee on Moral Education and, in England, a Standing Committee to oversee and implement the work of the Schools Council Project on Moral Education. He also suggested a Public Relations Liaison Committee which would bring the moral education activities into the public domain: 'stressing the importance', he said, 'of a morally educated public.' Victor then submitted the 'draft terms' he had been composing for his own Foundation.

On 21 February 1974 Victor wrote to W. K. Ferguson on the subject of Public Relations. Emphasising the need for giving people information on moral, religious and health education, he suggested that a Committee could use 'the most suitable media, possibly covering Television, the Press, Educational Correspondents of the Press, Films, Exhibitions and so on'; and he mentioned that the Gordon Cook Foundation had had its first Trustees' meeting on 18 February. We have no record of Victor's earlier meetings with Bill Ferguson, who was the HMI responsible for History and Modern Studies; this new subject, dealing with forms of government, citizenship and social issues, owed much of its successful development to Ferguson's pioneering work. In debate with such able and experienced officers as Earl, Lord and Ferguson, Victor could hardly fail to feel frustrated. His honest enthusiasm for moral, social and personal education would certainly have impressed them, but his determined advocacy of his own Plan and schemes, to be imposed on schools complete with teaching content and methods, could never gain the compliance he sought. He could not truly understand that the national bodies he was trying to influence had a distinct and peculiar place in the scheme of educational provision: they could advise, offer guidance and encouragement, but they could not dictate to either schools or local authorities; what was taught, and how it should be taught, could only be the product of complex, often lengthy processes of communication and research, with exchanges of ideas, experimentation, evaluation and consultations leading to a hoped-for acceptance of new approaches by teachers.

Knowing Bill Ferguson as I did, both as a colleague and a friend, I could easily imagine his somewhat brusque reception of Victor's proposals, and his impatience at Victor's persistent reiteration of his own convictions – expressed, it has to be said, in characteristically uncertain and somewhat disjointed speech. It was about this time that Victor and I met. He had written to me because he had read a piece I wrote about involving teachers in curriculum development and he wanted my support. He explained his ideas and told me that the officer who met him in St Andrew's House had roundly told him that there was no need for his ideas or (presumably) his money. I was able to assure him that I agreed with his aspirations, but in fact felt compelled to advise him that he would get nowhere unless he recruited the help of professional educators to give substance to the intellectual content of his schemes and practical validity to the work in schools. When he showed me his 'Plan' my reservations were even more pronounced. Victor frequently met with responses of that kind, and he was often discouraged; but his generous nature came to his rescue and he gradually became reconciled to the need for patience and tolerance. Before his close involvement with educators he had found it hard to grasp the truth that nobody in Britain could simply hand over to teachers a number of schemes like the blueprints he gave his engineer craftsmen and expect them to implement them in the classroom without judging their efficacy or, indeed, their educational value. Besides, his classroom schemes were naive, old-fashioned and badly designed for use with children. In time, however, he came to see the central importance of teachers in the design of practical materials, and especially to see that innovative curricula and methods could only become established through the efforts of planners, teacher trainers and educational advisers.

Chapter Four

The Plan and the Deed

Victor's Plan rested on the conviction that there is a range of 'simple', 'abiding', 'universal' moral principles which, once imbibed, stood by the individual as a permanent guide to how one should lead a good life. The Objectives he proposed as outcomes were unexceptionable to anyone who could be described as an ordinary, intelligent, well-meaning citizen interested in education. (Characteristically, however, he conceded that they might be 'amended as a Headmaster might think fit'.)

- That the young will have developed maturity of character, self-discipline and concern for the well-being and happiness of others
- That there will be a desire to care, to share and avoid selfishness
- That a clear code of standards for right thinking has been willingly accepted as given to pupils
- That a delight in the contemplation and production of things of beauty will have been instilled
- That they will value a good home and seek to take their part
- That they will seek good health in its widest aspects
- That they will face the challenge to youth today to fight the perverse influences undermining the character of the people
- That they have realised the dedication needed to their studies and their work, to make something worthwhile of life
- That the pupil may become a worthy, well-informed, responsible citizen

It is easy to point to tell-tale expressions that betrayed the impreciseness of his thinking and the rather antiquated notions he had embraced. What are we to understand by 'right thinking'? – or by 'value a good home'? – or by 'the challenge of youth today'? – or by 'the character of the people'? Of course teachers were understandably sceptical. Now, in the twenty-first century, teachers still hear hoary clichés of that kind. But we are now aware that it is an important part of teaching to encourage students to think about the meanings of our thoughts about life and to enquire into the nature of moral and social values. At the very least, we need to help our students to acquire and use the language of moral discourse. Not having that language, and having to rely upon his own (sometimes faulty) interpretation of what he read, Victor opened himself to criticism and even ridicule. His friend Jack Marshall has mentioned Miss H. Porter, a member of Robert Gordon's College junior school staff, who was 'sympathetic to Victor's endeavours albeit somewhat sceptical of some features of the "materials"'. Jack himself lent a kindly ear to Victor and tried to help him:

> Right from the start he agreed – at an intellectual level, at least – that there was an urgent need for a 'translation' of his classroom materials – but over the years it seemed clear to me that another part of his make-up stoutly resisted change in any significant way of the *ipsissima verba* once they had been shaped.

Not all of Victor's critical friends were so gently tolerant; but the majority of the many teachers who were persuaded to 'try out' his materials simply stopped using them, not having the heart to tell him bluntly that they were just too fuddy-duddy for the modern school.

A prime example was the 'Code' which he inserted in all the Topic Handbooks and Pupils' Log Books which comprised the bulk of the materials:

It is my duty to do my best.

1. To work willingly and to the utmost of my ability.
2. To be generous in thought, word and deed and to share my gifts.
3. To be honest and truthful in all things.
4. To be kindly to old people and children, and those in ill health.
5. Never to be a bully.
6. To be courteous and friendly with others without regard to race, creed or colour.
7. To be respectful to my teacher, clean, tidy and punctual.
8. To have self-respect and be clean in thought, word and deed, and avoid coarse expressions.
9. To be courageous and not afraid of difficulties.
10. To try and be forgiving.
11. To do kind things daily.

'The above', wrote Victor, 'are ways of thinking, attitudes for behaviour, cultivated by practice, guidance and explicit methods.' It is unclear what exactly he meant by 'practice', but certainly he could see beyond the mere chanting of 'rules' or slogans in the manner of the Edwardian Scout troop. He writes: 'How to instil the basic values is the burning question of today. To know what they are – honesty, kindliness, courage and the like – is not sufficient . . .'; and he applauds the sentiment that 'youth may fight what they consider to be injustice, whether it is economic, human rights or otherwise.' Had he lived into the nineties he would surely have supported the character-building activities now being employed in schools – such as mentoring, anti-bullying arrangements, youth councils, community projects, environmental improvement programmes and involvement in citizenship affairs. Beneath the old-world rhetoric and the golden-age assumptions there is a genuine understanding of the importance of making young people articulate about their roles in society and their personal responsibility for their own conduct. His idea of a personal Log Book in which a pupil could record day-to-day incidents relating to moral action reflects many similar modern devices for giving pupils continuous contact with their informal as well as their formal learning experiences in school.

Encouraged by sympathetic interest from some of the people he approached for advice, and a modicum of encouragement from a few professional educators – coupled of course with his own determined enthusiasm – Victor at last, at the beginning of 1974, set up the Gordon Cook Foundation – so called in memory of his beloved mother. It was established quietly by Trust Deed signed on 18 February at his lawyer's office and registered legally on 27 February. The Trust thus created was immediately granted the sum of £100,000 with the promise of further estate he might contribute during his lifetime or under his last will and testament. He described the Trust as 'relating to Citizenship Education for Character Development'. The preposition is important. In later years the Trust came to be known as the 'Gordon Cook Foundation for Citizenship *and* Character Development' and more recently the term 'Values Education' came to be substituted for 'Character Development'. Victor himself adopted 'Values Education' in place of 'Character Development', having been persuaded that this was a more modern and better description. In fact for Victor citizenship education as a form of 'Civics', learning about the mechanisms of government and political developments, never loomed large. His interest lay in the nurturing of the good citizen, who is in essence a good person, one who is aware of the importance of socio-political commitments but who is primarily dedicated to helping other people live more effective lives rather than changing the relations between individuals and government.

The first object of the Trust should be 'to advance, promote and carry out any aspects of education or allied activities likely to promote Character Development as hereinafter described'. This promised enlargement of the meaning of 'character development' is not really detailed. He stipulates as the second objective of the Foundation the provision of 'support, suggestions and information to teachers and parents relating to personal development of the child', and he offers a rationale which is at once sweeping and meticulously precise: 'Society renews itself through the schools. The endeavour would be to inculcate attitudes to life based on abiding values particularly during the early years when the foundations are laid.'

The full implications of this pronouncement escaped his trustees for many years, and even now, in the next century, it is likely that a majority of British educators would have serious reservations about the possibility of implementing Victor's aspirations. Society renews itself in a multitude of ways, schooling being only one of these; the schools are important vehicles for inspiring change, but so are the media, the churches, the myriad organisations that people form in order to influence the direction in which society moves forward. Again, how can attitudes be inculcated? They are the product, surely, of experience, of interaction with circumstances, as well as of teaching and learning. And what are the 'abiding values'? In the decades following the setting up of the Foundation it was common to scoff at the idea of there being values that everyone, or even most people, can take as true and universal. But Victor continued to work away at his self-appointed mission for the rest of his life: in the narrow sphere of his home, producing materials with his small team of helpers and trying to induce teachers to use them, and in the wider sphere encouraging a variety of innovative projects designed to advance the cause of explicit moral education.

His Deed of Trust stipulated a number of objectives which some of his trustees recognised as eminently practicable and worthwhile. He directed us to 'disseminate in every way possible the significant results of related research and development', and to 'promote Citizenship in its widest terms including Moral Education, Aesthetic Appreciation, Youth Activities, co-operation between the Home and the School with contribution from individual school subjects'. He listed several 'particular purposes' – 'but only for guidance to the Trustees' – that would further the original aims of the Trust. (These were based on the Articles of Association of the Farmington Trust.)

1. To promote methods of teaching Character Development in schools.
2. To co-ordinate the work in the school with leisure time pursuits.
3. To further the application in schools and the training in Colleges of Education of the Scheme of Character Development of the Child formulated through this Trust, a copy of which Scheme is attached hereto, or any other Plan whichever may be found most satisfactory.
4. To assess the results of pilot tests in schools by independent experienced researchers with power to modify the work in the light of experience.
5. To provide grants to Publishers to enable them to reduce prices of books or literature which would help to make known to the public in a popular manner useful, appropriate information within the scope of the Trust purposes.
6. To provide regular awards to any school or Centres of Education or any individual considered by the Trustees to have made in Great Britain a significant contribution to the aims of the Trust.

Although he never wavered in his conviction that moral education should and could be taught explicitly in schools, Victor characteristically inserted 'get-out' clauses which left his trustees virtually free to decide for themselves what should be done in the name of the Foundation: virtually free legally, that is, for he rightly assumed a strong moral obligation on their part to carry out his wishes in accordance with their own judgement as to what might be feasible and realistic. Ultimately, of course, the trustees could judge that the Trust purposes could not be carried out at all and were empowered to 'pay and make over the Trust Estate to any appropriate institution whose aims the Trustees consider would be nearest to the objects as set forth in these presents.' There were a number of such appropriate institutions (such as the Farmington Trust) and Victor was well aware of them. He also considered the possibility that the state might in the course of time undertake 'most or all of the functions of an Information Centre and other features of the Foundation', so he expressed the wish that we should consider, 'among other possibilities', devoting the income to financing memorial lectures on Character Development, 'preferably summarised with suggestions for practical application, printed and distributed widely to schools and elsewhere'. He was quite clear in his own mind what an information centre should do:

1. To provide continuous support and information for teachers.
2. To improve communications with and give support to Local

Authorities, Headmasters and Teachers with information, and to suggest programmes and syllabuses along with source material for classroom work, and to promote the availability of trained visiting teachers.

3. To collate existing material on this subject both from this country and abroad and form a library.

4. To establish Teachers' Working Parties in this field through existing Teachers Centres, with 'feed back' to an Information Centre.

5. Complementary to Religious Education, to assist locally with integrating as far as possible relevant work of the School, Church, Home and Youth Organisations.

6. To issue Bulletins or News letters regularly for distribution to Headmasters and Teachers suggesting source material, reference to latest research and development and examples of class work.

7. To assist in the formation of a Handbook of Citizenship considered in its widest sense which would be revised regularly.

8. To assist in the establishment of related courses for teachers 'in service' and student teachers in Colleges of Education.

9. To collaborate with the Central Council of Health Education for Schools or any equivalent body.

10. To provide liaison with English and Scottish Education Departments and with current Project work being undertaken in research and development.

11. To assist in stimulating more informed public opinion relating to the influences on the upbringing of children as given on Radio, Television, Films and Exhibitions.

In drafting his Deed of Trust Victor did not forget his other great enthusiasm, health education. It was listed as one of the objects for which he established the Trust, albeit as number six in a list of eight. Under the heading Health Education, he stipulated that 'the Trustees shall have power to support the teaching of Health Education in schools further to what is being done at present, and to give recognition and awards similar to that suggested for Character Development' – but he added that 'expenditure should be secondary to that of the Character Development work.' His reference to 'what is being done at present' pointed to what he himself was doing in his Topic Books and other materials issued to teachers. This consisted mostly of quotations from books and articles dealing with, for example, nutrition, mental health, sex-education, hygiene, 'temperate eating' and cleanliness. By the mid-eighties he was issuing more than twenty Topic Handbooks containing a variety of excerpts from the Health Education Unit and other organisations such as the New College of Health set up by Michael Young.

Victor proposed a simple structure of administration for the Trust: himself and four trustees appointed by himself. The trustees' 'main function', he proposed, would be 'that of a consultative nature deciding matters of policy'; clearly, it was his intention to continue to lead the work himself; and this is what happened during most of his life. The original trustees were contented to leave him alone with his small team of helpers in Countesswells House, painstakingly putting together the materials for the Topic Books. One, Sydney Davidson, was a retired surgeon; one, Bertram Tawse, was a highly successful civil engineer and businessman; and only two of us, Jack Marshall and myself, were professionally qualified as educationists. Sydney and Bertram were blissfully uninterested in Victor's life's work, but they were highly intelligent, genuinely good men, fond of Victor, and shrewd advisers on matters of business such as investments and the deployment of resources. Jack was of course a key figure: being the head of Aberdeen's most prestigious school, and a prominent and influential member of Scotland's educational elite, he gave the Foundation an important respectability among teachers. At that time I had just left being one of Her Majesty's Inspectors of Schools to become the Chief Educational Adviser in Lothian; I was also a member of the government's principal advisory body on education, the Consultative Committee on the Curriculum; and I was a fairly prolific writer on educational matters. Victor exploited both of us quite relentlessly as consultants. Fond as we were of him, Victor's continual lengthy phone-calls stretched our patience often to the limit.

Chapter Five

Political constraints

During the 1970s, a period in which Victor Cook managed the Foundation by himself, virtually without professional help, politicians, administrators and educators were preoccupied by three sets of problems: both in England and Wales and in Scotland, the dominant concerns were the raising of the school leaving age (ROSLA), the rapid expansion of comprehensive education, and the reorganisation of local authorities. All three developments produced significant changes in the management of schools, the provision of resources and the delivery of curriculum. These changes profoundly affected teachers' conditions of service and their capacity for meeting the educational needs of their pupils. They also had, in different ways, potential significance for the work of the Gordon Cook Foundation.

ROSLA had been announced by the government in 1964 but it was nearly ten years later that it was actually implemented. During the second half of the 1960s there were many projects aiming at the necessary changes in curriculum which would arise when teachers were faced with pupils aged 15 and 16 who were not destined to enter higher education. Nobody doubted that these pupils would be difficult to teach in their last two years of schooling; for this, and other reasons, teachers were almost wholly opposed to ROSLA. Their fears were strengthened by the realisation that – along with the effects of the bulge in the birth-rate – the increased numbers of pupils would not only result in bigger classes but would also reduce or constrain the extra resources they would need to cope with more non-certificate classes. But the most serious long-term worry was uncertainty about how these youngsters should be taught. It was universally agreed that the traditional academic curriculum was unsuitable. Subjects taught for the more academic pupils held little interest for pupils whose aspirations pointed forward to the time they could leave school and get a job. Formal teaching methods relying on 'talk and chalk' held no attraction for them. The schools were failing to catch the interest of many abler pupils too, who were leaving school to enter the world of work before they acquired certificates.

This was well understood by staff at national and local authority levels tasked with the production of new curricular practices. Years before ROSLA new schemes had been developed to make classwork more appealing and more appropriate. As early as 1955 the SED produced a report, *Junior Secondary Education*, which advocated new progressive approaches to give the less academic pupils more realistic experience and provide character training. In 1963 in England the Newsom Committee's Report, *Half Our Future*, proposed new 'child-centred' teaching for the less academic. In Scotland in the same year, the Brunton Report, *From School to Further Education*, proposed that courses for the 'non-certificate' pupils should be designed to exploit the 'vocational impulse' with 'centres of interest' and pre-vocational courses such as Retail Distribution and Office Studies. A number of schools developed successful courses along those lines. But in general the teachers, strongly supported by their unions, met the new ideas with indifference and even hostility. Soon after, however, two powerful bodies were set up to initiate and promote new curricular thinking: in England, the Schools Council (1964) and in Scotland, the Consultative Committee on the Curriculum (1965). These organisations had a profound effect on British education, producing a series of reports on every subject and area of school life, proposing whole new programmes of teaching and learning, conducting authoritative surveys of past and current practices and making recommendations on what should be taught and how, and how it should be assessed. By the time ROSLA was implemented there were ample materials for teachers to use, complete with syllabuses and assessment arrangements.

It proved to be well-nigh impossible, however, to overcome the natural reluctance of both parents and teachers to abandon the proven standards yielded by examinations and certificates; both insisted on the primacy of qualifications obtained by fair and reliable external examinations. In England, new-style examinations such as the Certificate of Secondary Education (CSE), carefully designed to assess competences required by jobseekers and workers, tended to be regarded as merely preliminary to more academic examinations; and in Scotland the Examination Board decided against introducing a specially designed certificate for less academic pupils, though in two of the larger regions a number of schools introduced school-based courses of the kind used in England. In the 1970s, however, differential banding of the Ordinary Grade Certificate allowed less academic pupils to gain conventional qualifications. None of these devices proved satisfactory, and it took many years of research and planning to produce the present highly sophisticated systems of examining and certification designed to cater equitably for the whole range of ability and career needs. ROSLA undoubtedly increased problems of discipline in schools, bringing an influx of reluctant learners into classrooms designed to cater for academic lessons and motivated pupils.

The reorganisation of local government was another powerful factor for change. Both in England and Wales and in Scotland, the number of local authorities was radically reduced, and the new larger regions introduced far-reaching reforms. They commanded much greater resources, and they quickly began to take greater control of the schools' staffing structures and system of curriculum delivery. Their greatest priorities were to expand and strengthen the comprehensive system: they introduced new ways of supporting teachers, providing more inspection and advisory staff, and making in-service training more accessible and more relevant. They built many new schools and provided enhanced technical resources for classrooms. Their major preoccupations in respect of curriculum were centred on improved provision: they aimed at smaller classes, better qualified teachers and more modern equipment. The expansion of comprehensive education was accompanied widely by efforts to achieve social equality, and this tended to preclude the development of curricula which stressed objectives not related to the basic skills and conventional attainment standards.

These developments did not bode well for Victor's personal crusade to introduce a major new responsibility for schools. His vision of Moral Education being given the status and resources accorded to the 'big' subjects like English, Science and Mathematics had little chance of being endorsed by the system, despite the fact that many people shared his central concerns. The Heath government was apprehensive that ROSLA, combined with rising unemployment and the decline of large sources of jobs in manufacturing, might lead to social disorder. ROSLA certainly made the unemployment figures more palatable politically, but other social changes were causes for unease: decline in religious commitment, evidence of rebelliousness among urban youth, the hedonism of the 'sixties culture'. Concerted efforts to improve the moral calibre of ordinary people seemed to be at least worth considering. It was in that context that Victor's approach to the Prime Minister was met with some approval.

Although his enthusiastic lobbying of influential people in England had won him some recognition as an advocate of moral education, he met eventually with bitter disappointment. It was difficult for him to admit to himself that his presentation of the merits of his plans and schemes failed to convince the policy-forming establishment in England; he was bewildered, and not a little angered, by the dawning realisation that he was being sidelined – courteously, no doubt, but firmly. A case in point was his proposal for a Public Relations Committee which would provide a forum for information and discussion on matters related to moral education, in particular the 'good and helpful work already carried out by the Education Authorities on both sides of the border'. His own work with schools in Aberdeen would of course figure in that kind of publicity. During 1973, however, he learned about the formation of a Social Morality Council, which seemed to have a close similarity to the organisation he had proposed, and to his intense annoyance heard that the minister, Mrs Thatcher, had given this Council a grant, while his own request for financial support had been ignored. Victor's recording of a telephone conversation with Mr Earl exhibits both his disappointment and his suspicions about the fidelity of the minister and her civil servants:

Telephone conversation between Mr Cook and Mr Earl on 17.9.73

Mr Cook.   I received a notice from the Social Morality Council that they have got a grant from the DES.

Mr Earl.   That is correct.

Mr Cook.   Does that grant refer to the proposals to Mr Heath?

Mr Earl.   This was organised some time ago and went through before your letter to Mr Heath was written. It arose out of a visit by a deputation from the SMC to Mrs Thatcher over a year ago.

Mr Cook.   When was the actual grant made?

Mr Earl.   The machinery was set in motion shortly after she saw them, that is, over a year ago.

Mr Cook.   But when was the grant approved?

Mr Earl.   Cannot tell you the exact month. Something of the order of nine months ago.

Mr Cook.   Are my proposals still under consideration?

Mr Earl.   Yes indeed.

32

Mr Cook. I asked for a meeting with those concerned, that is, yourself and any others, for a preliminary consideration of the situation. Hector Monro promised to do that but he said at the time that the others wanted to go further into the matter before our meeting. That was about six weeks ago. I have written one or two supplementary letters to Mr Monro preparing for our meeting, so that the position is that a grant may be given perhaps additional to this one if Mrs Thatcher, Mr Heath and the Department consider that it would be desirable.

Mr Earl. I think it is very doubtful because we are very reluctant to make grants, and although we have made a grant to the SMC, it is what we call a pump priming grant. I am not in a position to reveal the amount of the grant, but it is quite a small one, and only temporary to enable them to get started. They must rely on grants from independent trusts. We have given them enough to appoint an Officer for a year or so, but after this they will have to rely on what they get from trusts and so forth.

Mr Cook. My main objective has been to get a substantial grant from the Department because I personally feel how important it is that if it is to make a significant impact it must be done on a substantial scale with financial resources.

Mr Earl. I am afraid you will find the Department very reluctant to make any major grant for a whole variety of reasons.

Mr Cook. There are some other matters that I would like to discuss with you. You know you asked me originally if my proposals could be given to the SMC. I said it was alright, but of course any proposals or ideas of mine would still remain mine. No-one else could appropriate them without contacting myself because my papers are copyright. At the last meeting we had with Mr Blackham and yourself it was left a bit open. I was surprised to see, following this meeting, that the revised SMC Project incorporated about four or five essential points that were in the original Project, all exactly as I had them in my proposals, one of them being that it

33

would be complementary to Religious Education. Someone may have said that to them. But the point remains that this was not in the original Project and they had my proposals immediately afterwards.

Mr Earl.   I think this is coincidental. I think they had moved independently, but I cannot claim to know what went on in their own minds.

Mr Cook.   There was no reference to Religious Education in the first Project. They got my proposals which stated quite clearly it was complementary to Religious Education.

Mr Earl.   I think in fact the same idea had been in their earlier documents, although it was not in the Project sent to you.

Mr Cook.   The revised Project after our meeting was clearly seeking aid from the charitable institutions and decrying a Centralisation Grant. My proposal was quite different. I thought from the beginning, from the first time I saw Lord Belstead, that a substantial grant from the Department was needed. That was my idea and this is what I have been driving for all these years.

In your letter you mention to me 'I hope however that it will be possible for co-operation in the interests of Moral Education to continue to develop'.

Mr Earl.   I do still hope that it might be possible for some co-operation which would incorporate both your Project and the SMC's Project.

Mr Cook.   I was co-operating with them when I understood they were to be financed by charitable institutions – the same as the Farmington Trust, the same as the Foundation I am setting up myself. These are all voluntary. My own Trust would be co-operating with any others.

Mr Earl.   This is good news.

Mr Cook.   I understood that Mr Heath and Mr Monro were most enthusiastic with the suggestion.

Mr Earl.   The point is that Mr Monro, of course, has nothing to do with the DES. He is really the Parliamentary Under-Secretary for Scotland. Of course you will know better than I that there are all sorts of developments in Scotland. I understand in Scotland they are actively considering the Millar Report.

Mr Cook.   There is a tremendous vagueness yet. I have been in touch with a good many of the Colleges of Education. They are most anxious to know what to do and how to set about it precisely. This is one of my features. Besides the proposals, I have worked out a practical Scheme for the teachers. Because I am also running a business I have not had time as yet to develop this. The SMC say they would leave that to the teachers once it gets going. That is the whole difficulty. I have submitted one practical Scheme covering all the aspects and that is going a great deal further than what the SMC have done so far.

Mr Earl.   They are still in the process of setting up their Scheme.

Mr Cook.   I know that you have been sympathetic to me and very help-ful. I am not wanting to cause any trouble. I want to keep in close touch with you.

Mr Earl.   You will realise that between Scotland and ourselves especially on this line of business there is very little communication. My colleagues in Scotland are by law excluded from looking at Religious and Moral Education. I have in a sense no opposite number in Scotland I can talk to. My own concern is that these various efforts in Religious and Moral Education should co-operate rather than compete.

Mr Cook.   Co-operation is alright as long as one member does not appropriate the ideas of another. The ethics of this must be considered, most especially on this subject.

Mr Earl.   I will be travelling most of this week. Any message should be left at Norwich Office.

Mr Cook.   I will contact you later and let you know the developments.

The long-suffering Mr Earl was clearly doing his best to propitiate the irate Mr Cook without revealing that the much-vaunted Plan and Scheme was considered inadequate. Earl seems to have been virtually hounded by Victor: he was continually phoning him – and on at least one occasion he actually phoned him at home at a weekend – but Victor keenly appreciated his patience and courtesy. Nevertheless we must infer from the scant evidence we have – almost all from Victor's own archives – that there was a real intellectual fault-line between Victor's understanding and the civil servants' perceptions of what was feasible and permissible in the process of educational development and decision making. Victor was never able to grasp the central tenets of the official position in relation to school work: first, that government could not, by tradition and in principle, dictate to schools what they should teach; second, that in any case the propositions Victor was struggling to put forward were themselves too far from reality to be taken seriously; above all, there was considerable doubt that teachers and their political and academic advisers were prepared to accord much importance to moral education as a curricular subject, whether or not it was allied to religious education or 'citizenship' or any other area of schooling. This explains why even people sympathetic to the claims of moral education were reluctant to comply with his demands or even to give him open encouragement. Despite his frequent denials that his Scheme was 'ready made' and his assurance that head teachers would be able to adapt his work as they deemed appropriate, he was perceived to be touting materials that would be met with indifference or even antagonism in schools and teacher training colleges. Anyone interested in teaching morality would be better served looking to the work of Peter McPhail's project or the Farmington Trust (by now almost exclusively concerned with religious education) or the writings of John Wilson and others. Despite his persistence and his offers to make general financial donations, Victor's efforts to gain support from the establishment in England came to nothing. He came to see that his attention would be better concentrated on his own Foundation.

Chapter Six

Developments in moral education:
theory and practice

The Plowden Report, *Children and their Primary Schools* (1967), was the most influential source of educational guidance published in the twentieth century. It both reiterated the general principles of modern education and expounded the specific ideas underlying progressive child-centred education. Putting the child's own needs and nature at the heart of the educational process, rather than the perceived needs of society or the wishes of the parents, was innovative and bold, and the main thrusts of the Report's arguments were strongly supported by a formidable body of research. The central notion in Plowden was that effective primary education required a clear understanding of the developmental sequence undergone by children as they grow: each stage demands different teaching strategies, but each child must be carefully observed as an individual and diagnosed for such matters as rate of maturing and the social and personal factors which best facilitate the maturing process. Plowden Committee members were greatly indebted to the work of developmental psychologists, in particular to Jean Piaget. But the Report's references are all to intellectual and emotional growth; curiously, as we would notice nowadays, there is no mention of Piaget's important work on moral maturation. Indeed, moral maturation does not occur at all as a subject of relevance. This was no doubt because the members did not perceive moral education as an object of schooling as different in any meaningful way from religious education.

On the subject of religious education the Report frankly stated that members were divided in their views because of their personal beliefs. But the Report's silence on the teaching of morality in any form seems to indicate that members were largely agreed that religious education was the proper vehicle for explicit discussion of matters of right and wrong conduct. Moral development, they assumed, was entirely a consequence of emotional and social development. The child forms his sense of personal worth and his moral code from early experiences of acceptance, approval and disapproval. Out of an externally imposed rule of what is permitted arises a sense of what ought to be done and an internal system of control: 'in everyday terms, a conscience.'

The Report's naive and, to our eyes, inadequate account of moral development gives prior weight to the ethos of the school, supplementing the influence of the home, for moral education. This, it will be remembered, was the view taken by the members of the Millar Committee in Scotland; so also was the assumption that moral education could not feasibly be provided outside of religious education. The note of reservation appended to the Plowden Report by a distinguished group of members, including A. J. Ayer, D. V. Donnison, and M. Young, discusses religious and moral effects of schooling, reiterates the belief that the 'moral benefit' a child derives from his education 'will be a function rather of the whole atmosphere, and the personalities of the teachers, than of any form of homiletics'. One member of this group (we are not told who) suggested that parents should be given the option of enrolling their children for 'a secular course in moral and social education' as an alternative to religious education; but the majority doubted the viability of such a course, holding to the view that 'it is not easy to see what form the syllabus of moral and social education could take'.

There can be little doubt that the Plowden Report represents the prevailing view of moral education in the 1960s and 1970s; that is, that the school does have a responsibility for the moral growth of its pupils, but this cannot be done by means of explicit moral teaching. Piaget had made his own opinion clear: 'You cannot further understanding in a child simply by talking to him.' Children, he wrote, should be allowed to do their own learning. Teachers should involve pupils in situations where they themselves conduct experiments, pose questions, seek their own answers. Social interaction among the pupils themselves will enable them to see different points of view. (This, too, in modern eyes, is an inadequate solution: not being himself an educator, Piaget did not apparently understand how teachers can construct situations to control learning and to lead the child towards deeper comprehension and more potent use of language.)

Piaget's account of a step-wise growth in moral maturity was generally accepted as an early theory which needed to be elaborated. He argued that children progress from a 'pre-conventional stage' in which their moral judgement is 'heteronomous', based on obedience to 'authorities', their behaviour determined by rules and their need to avoid rebuke or punishment, to a 'conventional' stage, in which judgements are made autonomously, their behaviour derived in part from awareness that other people also have needs and valid opinions, and that 'being good' – living up to what is expected of them by parents and teachers and other authority figures – was a prime value in life. At this autonomous stage they realise that social stability, both in their own lives and in the wider community, depends on obeying rules and carrying out obligations, contributing to the 'good of all'.

Piaget's most important successor as a theorist was Lawrence Kohlberg, whose work during the 1970s is still being actively continued by many developmental psychologists. Kohlberg postulated a six-staged sequence of moral growth. For each stage it is possible to exemplify the highest level of moral judgement the child is capable of at that age. Moral action partly depends on moral judgement, he argued, since it requires the ability to see the consequences of your behaviour and to envisage the likely outcomes of your actions. In Stage One, the child has no consideration of motive, and behaves, as Piaget had earlier suggested, wholly in response to rules and possible sanctions. In Stage Two, there is an awareness that others have purposes and interests which may conflict with your own, and the knowledge that you may have to make concessions to get your own way: it is 'right' to 'exchange' to satisfy both your own and the other's interests. Stage Three brings awareness of other people's wants, and a desire to gain approval for doing 'what is expected of you'; for being 'loyal', 'obedient', 'trustworthy', 'honest'. (At this stage, Kohlbergian psychologists believe, it is productive to discuss these values and what they mean for human satisfactions and progress.) At Stage Four 'social stability' is recognised as a good, a desirable state, and value is placed upon adherence to rules, to duties, to service to the group or the community. At Stage Five the growing person is aware that values are not absolute but derive from a common need to act together, to talk out and resolve conflicting interests. Values are relative, but they should be upheld impartially because they are based on an implicit commitment to other people and to society, a social contract everyone ought to honour if human life is to be satisfactory. Stage Six is characterised by a rational belief in universal moral principles, a commitment to justice, to human rights; and this commitment is independent of the values of any particular community or group. Kohlberg conceded that few people could be expected to live entirely in accordance with all the ideals of Stage Six, but there are great exemplars in history (such as Gandhi, Martin Luther King, Nelson Mandela and Mother Teresa) and moral education should aspire to helping all young people to live up to the values exhibited in Stage Six. Like Piaget, Kohlberg stressed the importance of social experience for moral growth, but his faith in rational discourse was such that he empha-sised the value of discussing moral problems in which students explore the rights and wrongs of imagined actions relating to a narrative about someone's moral dilemma. Although it has been irreverently dubbed 'dilemma busting', this approach is still widely practised.

Other scholars in the moral education field were concerned with the elements of moral behaviour – what constitutes good conduct in life. The Farmington Trust Research Unit, under the direction of John Wilson, produced an important analysis which was widely used in teacher educa-tion. Wilson categorised virtuous behaviour and labelled each category by using the first few letters of Greek words. In his influential book, *Practical Curriculum Study* (1982), Douglas Barnes interpreted them as follows:

Phil. It is necessary to see other people as having equal rights to one's own.

Emp. In order to act morally one has to be capable of sympathetic insights into people's feelings and motives, including one's own.

Gig. This element in moral action refers to the possession of rele-vant information: we cannot act with full moral responsibility unless we are fully informed about the situation and the likely outcomes of our actions.

Dik. Moral action entails the possession of moral principles that guide our behaviour: habitual unreflective behaviour is not moral. These principles must be rational in the sense of being consistently and logically applied.

Phron. This element concerns the possession of principles that refer to ourselves.

Krat. Moral judgements alone are not enough: there must be the will to put them into effect.

Wilson addresses the question of how his abstract categorisation of the make-up of the 'morally educated' should be utilised in teaching. He does not at all question the validity of his account or the desirability of teach-ing the moral principles. His concern is to further the research, to test how children can best be helped to develop morally. He proposes six 'preconditions', such as 'emotional security' at home, linguistic ability, and ability to relate emotionally to other people. He rejects 'direct attempts to "teach values"'. He does, however, suggest twenty-two 'possibilities' for schools to try out: these include direct attempts to teach moral skills, and a number of activities which are now familiar. These comprise such approaches as allowing pupils a measure of 'self-government', group methods, mentoring, outdoor education, role-playing, what we now call 'service education' (for example, helping in the community), a measure of self-assessment, and teaching related to 'practical living' such as education in sex, marriage, infant care, careers and so on.

John Wilson's work, like that of Victor Cook, suffered to some extent from a prevalent distaste for 'moralising'. Many teachers were (and still are) averse to the imposition of moral values on pupils, however indirectly. In a pluralist society, they argue, nobody has a right to dictate to young people what is right or wrong about the way they and their parents choose to live. What Victor called the 'basic values' or the 'abiding truths' – which he assumed were 'non-controversial' – might not be seriously disputed. In all probability almost everyone will agree that it is good to be honest, to be fair, to help the sick, to respect other people's rights and so on. But there is no assurance that applications of core values – examples of how they operate in practice – will be taken for granted. Different perceptions, different interpretations, different emphases will always occur, and ensuing conflicts will cause disagreement, unease, hostility. In modern moral education the teacher sets out to assume a 'neutral chairman' position and allow the students to think their own way through a topic, making sure that they have the information necessary for them to understand the context and outcomes, and the language needed to permit rational discussion. The identification of moral principles, or core values, is only a beginning: what the teacher can do is to help students to analyse the factors which lead to moral decisions. That is why the use of narratives presenting moral dilemmas is a favourite approach. Even then, however, different teachers will adopt different stances, some maintaining neutrality and others feeling obliged to promote certain moral views. Teachers trained to conduct moral discourse will usually achieve impartiality, but there are teachers who are so strongly committed to particular religious or political beliefs that they are unsuited for moral education courses.

By the 1970s it was firmly established in British educational policies that the 'direct' or 'explicit' teaching of moral values was not practicable as a separate or distinct activity in schools. Religious education had long been acknowledged as the proper vehicle for the explication of moral principles as these emerge from the Christian ethic, and it had become common to refer to 'religious and moral education' as an integrated discipline. Apart from that subject (known as RME), the school was deemed to have a general responsibility for the moral growth of pupils; the general perspective was that pupils should encounter values in social education and in guidance sessions, and also in subjects like English and History where human conduct was an object of study. In 1972 the Schools Council Moral Education Curriculum Project, which Victor Cook had been instrumental in setting up, produced curriculum materials under the title *Lifeline* which were designed to be used throughout the normal curriculum for the purpose of stimulating discussion of issues of conduct; it utilised role-play, creative writing, art work and other activities to help the discussion of moral problems. The director, Peter McPhail, and his team reported that their survey showed that 70 per cent of pupils expected some help from school in moral matters, and they produced a scheme for analysing pupils' responses to questions about how they would deal with specified everyday incidents. This project had little effect on the curricula of most schools; nor did another project, the Humanities Curriculum Project, which involved 'neutral' discussion of social and political issues, some of them regarded as controversial at the time.

Victor Cook's work made no impact on the contemporary debates about the role of moral education in the curriculum. This was, in the main, because the subject failed to arouse interest among educators or politicians or their numerous advisers. It was also because he seems to have given up the hope of influencing the course of events in the wider sphere, concentrating his efforts on the production of classroom materials; but these, as we shall see, were conceptually weak and badly designed, and he could find only a tiny number of schools prepared to use them. This may be judged particularly unfortunate, with hindsight, because in essence they had a certain potential for contributing to the promotion of moral education, as can be discerned from the book he produced to explain his Plan and provide a rationale for his work. (It was, of course, characteristically produced in an amateurish form, hand-typed and bound in dull black by a local printer.) The book represents at least twelve years of painstaking work, almost wholly Victor's; almost every page of his own copy has scribbled notes and emendations which indicate the man's diffidence and determination to get things right. Again and again I tried to persuade him to have it properly printed and disseminated but always got the same answer – it wasn't finished. I often thought of offering to revise it – to render his ideas into more modern, more relevant language, but my heart failed – that would have been an unkind attack on his very reason for living.

Nevertheless, given a more modern dressing, most of his objectives would nowadays be accepted as worthwhile, especially by people with normal perspectives on the upbringing of children; people, it may be said, like Victor himself. As I point out in Chapter 4, the stipulations he made were expressed in a somewhat antiquated style, and they were imprecise and over-generalised as pedagogical goals; but so are many of the observations made by respected opinion formers (the popular philosophisers whose writings Victor studied and quoted). And they are, most of them, still proposed as desirable outcomes of modern schooling. 'Maturity of character' and 'self-discipline' are often claimed to be attributes that must emerge from the educational policies of politicians. 'Concern for the well-being and happiness of others' is a respectable aspiration in many a school mission statement. 'A desire to care, to share and avoid selfishness' frequently occurs in various forms in sermons and prize-giving speeches. And Victor's emphasis on the educational importance of 'a delight in the contemplation and production of things of beauty' would still meet with universal approval. In general, then, Victor's aims represented the way most ordinary benevolent lay people would express their hopes for their children's education. So also would the third requirement in his decalogue: 'a clear code of standards for right thinking' (though he would have won very little applause if he had spelled out exactly what he meant by 'standards' and 'right thinking'!).

It is widely thought today that children should be introduced to a 'code' of values; but what these ought to be, and how they should be 'taught', are deeply problematical. But it is scarcely relevant in this context that Victor's own personal values would not coincide easily with those of modern liberal-minded people. The 'code' he and his assistants set out to transmit in their classroom materials embraced many of the social and moral values commonly cited today as comprising 'good citizenship'. Other values promoted in the materials would need to be brought up to date by modern teachers. The value of 'a good home' is all very well, but we would now want a much wider and more socially acceptable interpretation of what constitutes a good home. Again, the sentiments of 'dedication' to 'studies' and 'to make something worthwhile of life' (the protestant work ethic) are commonplace today, though the language echoes Samuel Smiles.

Victor's seventh commandment, that youth must face the 'challenge' to 'fight the perverse influences undermining the character of the people' reads like an extract from Lord Reith's diary, but in fact it is a direct borrowing from an essay, 'Education, Culture and the Social Order', published by the World Education Fellowship in The New Era (March 1970) which strongly appealed to Victor. It was written by Dr K. C. Saiyidain, a former education adviser to the government of India. Victor fits the quotation into the context of a plea for citizenship education for secondary schools:

For Youth today, two essential needs are:

(a)   The seeking and acceptance of abiding values.
(b)   A Challenge.

What is the challenge for the adolescent? Dr Saiyidain maintained, 'Is it not the challenge to fight the perverse influences of today? Youth is born to fight and, perhaps never before in the history of mankind, has a greater challenge been offered by destiny to men of charity, courage and goodwill to fight against the evils and perversions of thought that are poisoning the sources of our essential humanity.'

Victor also quotes from an article in the *Illustrated London News* by Sir Arthur Bryant, the historian and biographer:

Herein lies the key to our future as a people. It is on our national character that we depend, and if we lose it, we shall perish. Other of our inherited assets we cannot take with us into the new world, but, whatever we have lost or are about to lose, if we preserve our character as a people, we shall live on, and that character is in danger today.

What Victor actually wanted the schools to do in the fight for the national character is obscure; his own rhetoric is as hazy as that of his mentors. His understanding of political philosophy was minimal, derived mainly from the daily press and weekly popular journals. But his aspirations are boldly declared: he hoped that schools could help develop 'character' by teaching 'the Pauline injunction for personal development by cultivating the Fruits of the Spirit – love, joy, peace, patience, kindness, faithfulness and self-control'. This is the essence of Victor Cook's nebulous educational doctrine: for him, moral education is about helping young people to love their fellow human beings.

Much of Victor's rationale for moral education was reflected in the report of the Munn Committee, *The Structure of the Curriculum* (1977), one of the most important educational documents of the twentieth century. Sir James Munn's committee argued that schools must take responsibility for helping pupils to make sense of their personal circumstances and give them opportunities to exercise individual responsibility. Social values must be cultivated in an 'effective moral as well as a social education'. Although society itself is deeply divided on a whole range of moral and social issues, schools need to help pupils to become mature and humane individuals. Pupils' emotional and moral natures, their attitudes and values, many qualities of mind and character are prime concerns of the school. Pupils need to be helped to develop 'dispositions' to be concerned for other people and to show compassion for them, to be tolerant and fair, self-reliant and hard-working. A commitment to certain attitudes and values, including the values implicit in the corporate life of the school, should be an important outcome of education. The committee proposed moral education as a 'mode of activity' constituting an essential area of learning. Although they followed the tradition of assigning the care for morality to 'Religious and Moral Education', they recognised that 'moral questions are logically distinct from and are not reducible to religious questions.' In moral education pupils 'may be expected to explore the basis of human conduct, including their own, to reflect on personal and social problems, and to appreciate that moral issues are not to be settled by simple appeals to authority... but rather by adducing valid reasons, which are open for discussion, for or against particular kinds of behaviour.'

Victor Cook might have been expected to applaud the Munn Committee for putting forward the definitive case for moral education. Unfortunately, from Victor's point of view, they fell short of proposing a separate curricular role for moral, as distinct from religious, education. Religious and Moral Education was certainly placed in the Core Area, the subjects to be taken by all pupils, but although the report points out that there are valid distinctions it suggested that the work of distinct (or explicit) moral teaching should be spread over all subjects. All teachers must contribute through their specialisms, and the school ethos, reflected in the informal and 'hidden' curriculum, should play a central part. This was not satisfactory to Victor. All through the 1970s he had been doggedly preparing and issuing topic sheets, 'guidance' and classroom worksheet materials, regardless of the criticism and indifference of teachers and the scepticism of his advisers. This was no doubt because the work had become essential to his purposes in life, but it was also because he was deeply convinced of the need for explicit and methodical moral teaching.

Chapter Seven

The failure of the pedagogy

It has been shown in Chapter 6 that most of the objectives set out by Victor Cook for his Plan would, on the whole, be regarded as acceptable by the majority of the lay public in his own time, and even by professional educators today, despite the awkwardness of his style of presentation. But it has to be said that his efforts to establish moral education as an acknowledged and separate area of the curriculum were almost wholly unsuccessful. By the end of the 1970s this was becoming evident to all who had been trying to help him. The reasons for the failure of Victor's work are fourfold: firstly, the education system's preoccupations left no room for serious consideration of an innovation that seemed to most teachers to be peripheral; secondly, Victor's methods and materials were technically poor (though they were precursors to approaches being vigorously pursued today); thirdly, the management of the campaign was weak and largely ineffective. But above all, his materials exhibit a general outlook that was inimical to modern views about life and society. They were excessively didactic, assuming that they could be forced on to children's consciousness; they were authoritarian, condescending, and unrealistic.

As we have seen in Chapter 5, the education system throughout Britain was preoccupied by the consequences of the raising of the school leaving age, by the expansion of comprehensive schooling, and by the resource problems raised by the regionalisation of local government. Partly because of these changes there was a decisive shift of educational priorities. Courses suited to the interests and needs of 'less academic' pupils (that is, young persons due to leave school at 16 and enter the world of work) were being designed and taught, and new technologies were being exploited to raise standards in literacy and numeracy. In 1976 James Callaghan, the new Labour Prime Minister, launched the Great Debate in his famous Ruskin College speech: he declared that schools were failing to meet their pupils' needs for training in skills required to equip them to find useful jobs and work productively in industry and commerce. This resulted in new governmental emphases on preparation for working life: more teaching of literacy and numeracy skills, more careers guidance, and new forms of work experience. These priorities were continued in the 1980s by the Conservative government led by Margaret Thatcher. The Technical and Vocational Education Initiative (TVEI) and the Youth Training Scheme, launched in 1982–3, with their emphasis on basic and practical skills, promoted utilitarian values supporting the national drive to improve the economic performance of the country; nearly everyone agreed we must work harder in education to help earn our living as a nation.

Thus at a time when Victor Cook's Foundation was attempting to persuade teachers to teach more personal and social education they were being urged by authorities to give higher priority to English Language, Mathematics and Science, and to make time for work experience and the kind of social competence needed to perform better in interviews. This is not to say that there was no interest in the teaching of moral and social values, but teachers who were willing to use Victor's materials did not find them in tune with the prevailing ethos: these were, in the main, teachers in primary schools, and in the secondary schools the teachers with responsibility for 'guidance', which concentrated on curriculum advice, careers guidance and – to a much lesser extent – on personal problems raised by individual pupils. In many schools some weekly time was assigned to the discussion of issues likely to cause problems, such as alcohol and drug abuse, smoking and sexual behaviour. A number of secondary teachers did try out Victor's Topic Worksheets, but they seldom asked for more. From the beginning of his personal crusade, of course, Victor accepted that his work should be subject to critical scrutiny and adaptation. He often made this admission with reluctance, but gradually, through the seventies and eighties, he came to understand that the most satisfactory approach would be to enlist practising teachers, advisers and teacher trainers as allies in the pursuit of experimentation in a field that was new to practically everyone concerned.

Exactly what was faulty in the materials and methods promulgated by Victor and his small team of associates was made clear in an evaluation project his trustees commissioned shortly after his death. As trustees and friends we were not disposed to challenge Victor's life's work, but when we were charged with the direction of the Foundation we felt it necessary to have a clear understanding of its value and how it should be developed. The evaluation was undertaken by a team of four members of staff of the Northern College, Aberdeen, a teacher training institution, now part of Aberdeen University: Dorothy Browne, Audrey Allan, Margaret Forbes and Lynn Gee. All were experienced teachers and experts in teacher train- ing, curriculum design and teaching methods. They were all committed to the promotion of values education, so their views could be counted on to be kindly rather than hostile. Many of the critical comments in the evaluation reports echoed observations I and others had made personally to Victor in an endeavour to help him modernise his approaches and materials; but coming from these authoritative educators the assessments could be relied upon to be true to the prevailing principles of Scottish teachers.

In regard to the rationale for the Plan which Victor compiled and emended over two decades, from 1967 to about 1985, the evaluators agreed that the values proposed in the materials were in the main acceptable. They commended Victor's 'good will' and 'strength of purpose', but they all felt that his voice was that of a bygone age, worthy but out of date. As Margaret Forbes wrote, 'I find it difficult to dismiss the materials out of hand but they are needing to be rewritten to suit the changing needs in our schools today' (this was in the early nineties). They agreed that Mr Cook had worthily 'explored the need for values education'; but they were compelled to point out that while they could applaud his strong desire to know about children and their schools, 'the fruit of his search, whilst containing much that is correct and insights widely accepted in education, lacks the coherence of real understanding.' They felt, as Dorothy Browne put it, that his statements of principles, aims and objectives were 'based on a world view that many teachers of the 60s and 70s would have found narrow or at least tending to be so'.

The evaluators carefully scrutinised the materials that Victor and his team had produced: more than 200 'Topic Handbooks', with 'kits', Log Books, worksheets and games for use in the classrooms of primary and early secondary schools. These varied widely in quality, but the evaluators agreed that most of them were unsuitable for modern teachers. They were 'rather dull and uninspired', 'highly prescriptive', with 'sexual stereotyping' and a clearly apparent social bias, catering rather for children of higher social status and greater ability than the average. Many of the scenarios designed to stimulate discussion were 'not appropriate', not authentic portrayals of modern life. The evaluators particularly disliked the topics based on an American book, *The Tuckers*, a long-time favourite of Victor's. Published in 1959, it was out of print and had a number of drawbacks:

1. It reflects the social attitudes of USA circa 1952.
2. A Scottish child today would have difficulty in relating to the family lifestyle portrayed.
3. There is sexual stereotyping in evidence.
4. Copies are not available.

It was characteristic of the amateurish nature of the enterprise that Victor's team thought it feasible to 'use' *The Tuckers* stories by providing summaries and subtending discussion points about incidents, characters and so on.

Another form of discussion materials they issued was a strip cartoon, cleverly drawn by one of the team; it was about a family, the McSmiths, a take-off of *The Tuckers*; indeed, Victor occasionally inclined towards plagiarism in his use of other people's writings, though he made clear his intention of seeking permissions. In fact, however, all the materials he issued could easily pass for experimental, 'research-type' matter which was safely within the law. The scenarios of the McSmith materials were, the evaluators pointed out, like those of *The Tuckers* materials in being too little related to the real lives of the primary school children for whom they were written. But they thought the idea was a good one and could well have been extended in more professional form beyond the few actually issued.

It was, however, the methodology that was found most wanting by the evaluators. The whole scheme was fragmentary – produced as it was piecemeal, as ideas occurred to Victor or his helpers and issued more or less at random to anyone who had agreed to accept them. There was too much literal comprehension work, too much emphasis on cognitive development, not enough opportunities to bring the children's own experience to bear on the topics. Much of the follow-up work in values required copying from the blackboard, 'an activity', it was pointed out, 'that proves to have little to offer in the promotion of learning'. There was too much teacher-dominated discussion. In the course of the suggested time allocations – one hour twice weekly – a child would absorb a set of predetermined values: 'This is far removed from the methodology favoured today. No experiential learning is used in the Foundation's approach.' The structure of the topic notes was repetitive, and took too little account of varying levels of ability in a class. The selection of stories was too narrow. Questions asked and discussed did not reflect the interests of real children. As Dorothy Browne summed up, the methodology was 'unacceptable in the light of modern approaches to Primary Education'.

The evaluators found some features of the scheme commendable. The idea of giving each child a Log Book was thought attractive, though in practice they were no more than blank paper and there was insufficient guidance offered as to how they should be used. (Nowadays the use of similar materials is widespread in North American schools.) The themes listed for discussion were mostly interesting, but on the whole, they pointed out, modern primary teachers do not need that kind of help – they can arouse interest in discussing countless incidents within the school day. The themes listed for 'World Studies' were thought to be 'widely relevant and commendable', and the information provided would be useful to teachers who wanted to use the outlines in the way they were presented. But few teachers would want to use them in that way, on the basis of bare accounts of institutions and movements. Teachers would wish to generate enthusiasm for citizenship in global terms and for commitment to taking responsibility for the community, the environment and the maintenance of world peace and cooperation. World Studies should have an affective dimension, to give pupils 'a feeling for the global community'. Again, the methodology was seen to have a crucial weakness: the materials and indeed the whole approach catered for 'children within a limited range of ability and social background'. This criticism was generally applied to all the methods and materials used by Victor and his team. Also, they were thought to be monotonous, over-intellectualised and lacking in the kind of emotional excitement the subject demanded.

The most severe criticisms are put forward by Lynn Gee in her evaluation of the materials for S1 and S2. Apart from the same kind of strictures levelled by her colleagues on the dated and biased nature of the materials and the traditional and monotonous methodology, she writes with uncompromising frankness about the shortcomings of the moral teaching revealed in the scheme:

The teacher is seen as having 'received' moral truth which is imparted to the pupils, who will be 'receptive' to this new knowledge. This is an old-fashioned and very middle-class view which undermines the pupils' abilities to reach their own moral conclusions, even if they differ from those of the teacher. The material also tends to brand people as certain 'moral types' who are beyond 'redemption', eg there is a section on classroom behaviour which tells pupils to 'Beware of the swot, the class clown, the bully etc.' The treatment of 'Tolerance' is simplistic in that it implies that we do not tolerate [exercise tolerance] between people simply because these differences have not been properly explained to us. If this were so, then problems such as racism or sexism would have an obvious solution. Perhaps the most alarming aspect of the material is that it often confuses ordinary everyday problems with 'moral issues'. For example, to be ill is viewed as having low moral fibre . . .

The example she singles out for condemnation is a sequence in which the illness of a mechanic's wife sets off a chain of events which results in someone not getting a job because a bus did not turn up to take them to an interview. The moral, she writes, 'is stated thus. "One person ill somewhere may start up a chain of events which may hurt someone they've never even heard of!" It does seem positively harmful to try and instil this kind of attitude.'

Lynn Gee's main conclusion, it seems to me, sums up the fundamental weakness of Victor's moral teaching: it fails to take account of the nature of the children it addresses: 'It sees them as empty vessels, waiting to be filled with right moral attitudes, and all will be well.' The psychology is essentially mistaken. Pupils are constantly trying and testing out different interpretations of moral judgements; in adolescence particularly, they have their own personal conflicts which cannot be resolved by merely telling them what is right and what is wrong. They need to be helped to analyse their feelings and attitudes and to reach a better understanding of themselves; and above all their self-esteem needs to be built up. As Lynn Gee perceptively put it in her report, 'it is only from a standpoint of self-knowledge and self-esteem that an individual might begin to develop and accept certain moral attitudes as being right.'

Of course the fact that Victor's scheme was external to the education process he was trying to influence was a further difficulty. As Margaret Forbes wrote:

the personal role of the class teacher is a vital one; the interpersonal relationship with the individual child is a continuing one. Moral education cannot be effectively imposed by encoded didactic materials. ... The need for professional judgement is part and parcel of the teacher's daily work and it is bound up with knowing the children intimately as individuals/group/class, responding to the needs of all in their varying situations. By careful forward planning and preparation the class teacher can build in attitudes and values to the work of the class. In this way they are part of a whole and, therefore, have more meaning for the child. This also avoids the stereotyping which can result from the 'moral tale' approach.

If Victor Cook had had access to the wisdom of experienced educators like these – if he had commissioned expert evaluators to analyse his work and point the best way forward – the story of his life's work would have been very different. But he was entrenched in the thinking he had acquired from out-of-date psychologists and traditionalist educational writers, reinforced by the folklore recounted in the newspapers, and he was forced to follow his own lonely path, with a small team of assistants who could only carry out his hesitant and often inept instructions. Unfortunately none of his trustees was able to influence him sufficiently to help him until well into the 1980s. His frequent frustrations were due to frequent failures. He spent large amounts of his money having materials prepared, duplicated and sent out to schools, only to find that teachers, by and large, simply stopped using them. His correspondence includes many letters complaining, in his courteous style, that head teachers had received hundreds of copies of his handbooks, worksheets and log books, and had not been able to give him evidence that they were in use.

Another source of failure was the inadequate model of dissemination and development at his disposal. He had no option but to adopt what is called a 'centre-periphery' model, his rooms in Countesswells House being the hub, sending out information and materials to individuals, mostly head teachers, who were expected to distribute them to teachers. His first approach to me occurred when he read accounts of the methods I was using as a staff inspector for English and chairman of an official Central Committee. This was known as a 'proliferation of centres' model: my central team set up an Information Centre, while we visited education authorities, spoke to teachers and set up, through them, Local Development Groups (LDGs) who received materials, assessed them, adapted them to suit their own circumstances, and ensured that they were used by teachers in their area. At every point the LDGs and individual teachers were free to ally themselves to the central team to evaluate and develop the methodology and the materials. For some years Victor had been urging government officials to consider setting up a Centre for Information and Development in Citizenship and Character Development, but he had met a blank wall of indifference. The real success factor was one that Victor did not have: the powerful backing of government with the energies of a team of well-informed and strongly committed leaders.

Countesswells House

Burnett and Reid's Office in Aberdeen – where the Trustees
began to meet in 1974

Marianne Knight,
former Foundation
Secretary

Irene Brown,
present Foundation
Secretary

Opposite:
Some Reports issued
by GCF in the 1990s

Sheila Bloom,
Chief Executive,
IGE (UK)

'The Maine Group': (left to right) Frank Lennon, Anne Macintosh, Mike McCabe,
Stewart Jardine, Gordon Jeyes, Tom Wilson, Bill Gatherer, Judith Sischy, Mary McLaughlin,
Sheila Bloom

Chapter Eight

The way towards public acceptance

The development of Victor Cook's perceptions of his work coincided with a gradual increase in his trustees' advice and assistance. As Victor came to realise that he would have to look outward to seek support and cooperation from a wider circle of professional educators, he began to profit from a more active participation in the Foundation's business by one or two of his trustees. The first meetings of the Board of Trustees consisted of brief accounts from Victor of what he had been doing; all the 'progress reports' were written by himself; Professor Farqhar MacRitchie, designated Secretary to the Foundation, took no active interest in its actual educational work. Victor was still, well into the 1970s, engaged in correspondence with such notabilities as Sir Walter Coutts and Professor Williams of the Farmington Trust and the HM Inspectors from the Department of Education and Science in London and the Scottish Education Department in Edinburgh. My own relationship with Victor matured into a quiet friendship which survived various attempts by me to help make his work more acceptable to the educational world at large. I believe the experience of Jack Marshall, the other educationist on the Board of Trustees, was similar. More and more as the decade progressed, Victor sought feedback and reassurance from the teachers who agreed to try out his materials. Terms like 'testing' and 'evaluation' entered his vocabulary. But this did not mean that he abandoned his determined efforts to introduce his Plan and get his materials into the classrooms. The assistance he received from his small band of part-time helpers became more important to him; they gradually became associated with the devising and design of materials; but they were still very definitely assistants, under the command of Victor himself.

In 1979 I arranged for him to meet an Adviser in Guidance, Janette Fancey, a member of my staff in Lothian. She organised a meeting in Edinburgh at which Victor heard from Guidance teachers what they did and which topics they most wanted to discuss with their pupils. At last he was meeting teachers who were genuinely interested in moral and social values and had time set aside for them to pursue an active consideration of many of the topics he himself was trying to introduce: topics like the use of alcohol, nutrition, relations within the family and so on. Acquaintanceship with teachers and pupils matured his understanding of their aspirations and problems; having lived his life as a bachelor, isolated with his mother in Countesswells House, leaving in the mornings to go to work in the business, coming home at night to eat, play his piano and read his books, he seldom even saw a child. But the young people he was now meeting found him charming. Both the children and their teachers saw him as 'a nice old boy'; a bit old-fashioned in appearance and in speech, he was always kindly and courteous in manner. He seldom spoke about himself and he was never inquisitive about people. He much enjoyed listening to teachers talking about their jobs, and they knew that his interest was genuine.

The widening of Victor's outlook was greatly enhanced by a number of new allies he met through the agency of his trustees. In 1977 I was invited to address a World Convention of the International Reading Association in Louisville, Kentucky, and extended my visit to the States to meet some leaders in Educational Research and Development (R and D as it was called) in Washington DC. R and D was now a huge and growing activity throughout the world, and especially in America. The Russians' astounding achievement with Sputnik had inspired a great burst of reform in the teaching of English, Science and Mathematics as the Americans struggled to catch up, and throughout the sixties and seventies more attention was being paid to the development in students of the so-called 'soft skills' – the capacity for cooperating with others, leadership, competence in personal relationships and ability to think with clarity and imagination. For teachers this required training in values education: developing in the young the ability to discuss and clarify values, and dispositions to resolve conflicts, care for others and be emotionally committed to fair play, compassion and honest conduct. I had long admired the work in this field of Professor Urie Bronfenbrenner, and I visited Cornell University to meet him, discuss our mutual concerns and tell him about the Gordon Cook Foundation. The following year I took advantage of Bronfenbrenner's visit to Glasgow to deliver a public lecture, and introduced him to Victor, who came to hear his address. Victor and I then accompanied Urie and Liese Bronfenbrenner on a motor tour of Scotland, along Loch Lomond, through Perthshire and the Grampians to Aberdeen, where they spent a few days as Victor's guests in Countesswells House. It was a very successful and friendly meeting, and the two older men, so different in upbringing and experience, found real pleasure in one another's company. Characteristically, Victor thereafter took to referring to Bronfenbrenner's book, *Two*

Worlds of Childhood, and mentioning that he was 'a personal friend and supporter of our work'. Another influential acquaintance was Sister Pia Nazareth, a prominent teacher trainer in New Delhi and General Secretary of the All-India Association of Catholic Schools. Her book, *A Child's World of Values*, had come to Victor's attention, and in the course of a correspondence he had agreed to give her financial assistance to attend a conference on moral education in the USA and invited her to visit the Foundation. Consequently I met her in Edinburgh and took her and a colleague, Sister Maria Waples, to dinner. Sister Pia later visited Aberdeen where she joined the trustees for lunch and – as Victor later wrote – she 'examined our work at a School and took copies of our Plan and Topic Handbooks to India to collaborate with us in the future'. An important result of our association with Sister Pia was that, by chance after a conference at the Vatican, she met Bart McGettrick and told him about the Gordon Cook Foundation. When he got home he contacted me to ask about it, and subsequently became a member of the Foundation's Board of Trustees. As principal of St Andrew's College of Education and a very prominent educationist he proved to be a great asset to our work.

In 1981 I organised a conference in Edinburgh on the subject of Responsibility Education. This was a term I then favoured to describe teaching and other educational activities designed to give pupils moral understanding and dispositions towards self-reliance, caring for others, cooperation and what is now called 'moral courage' – being able to 'stand up for what you believe to be right'. I had set up a Study Group to look into the subject, and more than eighteen months later it was ready to report back. I had also commissioned two papers on the subject from two distinguished young academics at Edinburgh University: Dr Alex Sharp, an educational sociologist, and Dr George O. B. Thomson, an educational psychologist. The Study Group consisted of Brian Ashley, Director of the School of Community Studies at Moray House College of Education (now the Faculty of Education at Edinburgh University), and his fellow members were my colleague Janette Fancey, Dr Paquita McMichael of Moray House, and Macdonald Wilkinson, a community education officer in Lothian. The group's report was powerful and wide-ranging, and the academic papers were scholarly and insightful; they proved to be particularly appreciated in America, where they were published in the journal of the School of Education at Indiana University (*Viewpoints in Teaching and Learning*, 1981).

The sixty participants at the conference represented preschool, primary, secondary and further education, and there were people from social work departments, the Christian Education Movement, and teacher training departments of the universities. The geographical spread included Strathclyde, Lothian, Fife and Perthshire. Feedback after the conference was positive: the majority found it stimulating, even inspirational, for while the issues we discussed were closely relevant to current concerns many of the ideas were new to practising teachers; some found the subject matter daunting as well as exciting.

The questions I posed to the discussion groups had also been given to the speakers, so that they could address the main issues:

1. Is the school as an institution capable of providing wide opportunities for the taking of responsibility by pupils, staff and the community?
2. How far is the school capable of demonstrating open government and full participation in decision-taking?
3. What sorts of practical steps could teachers take to implement Responsibility Education in the 3 areas of Pedagogy, Curriculum and Institution?
4. What can educators do to reassert the importance of Moral Education alongside exam-orientated, instrumental education?
5. Is there an incompatibility between the hierarchical structure of schools and Kohlberg's ideas of 'justice and the just community'?
6. To what extent might approaches such as the 'Moral Dilemmas Test' be used as the basis of 'teaching' moral values?

For a considerable number of the participants these were issues they had not hitherto been accustomed to consider in their everyday lives. The speakers and their supporting papers were informative, introducing them to concepts and terminology which – if not altogether novel – were certainly challenging. The last three questions in particular fell outside the experience of most of the teachers. They found the term 'moral education' rather strange, and they were newly introduced to the theories and activities associated with Kohlberg. The 'moral dilemmas' approach aroused much interest.

This conference and the report (*Responsibility Education: Towards a Definition*) received no attention in the press and did little to change the direction of educational development in Scotland. Yet it did, I believe, have a beneficial influence on the participants and the teachers who were able to read about the papers. While it cannot be claimed that Victor Cook came away from the conference a changed man, he was clearly impressed: he learned some significant things which must have helped him in his work. Firstly, he was reassured that he was not alone in according moral education a high place in the educational scene: here were professionals from schools, social work departments and universities who seriously wanted to ally themselves with the work of the Foundation. He was made more aware, too, that moral education could take many forms: as a subject it was wide-ranging, complex and problematical, highly controvertible, even contentious in its implications; above all, perhaps, it was not explicable in the simplistic terms he was accustomed to employ in his own writings. Importantly, it was evident that his own endeavours were not really adequate to the great purposes he had conceived for himself. He must continue to seek and work with allies, not only in the few schools to which he had been given access but also throughout the whole system: we needed educators to undertake research and experimentation, and we needed academic scholars to help clarify the conceptual problems we faced; importantly, we needed the active support and colleagueship of people whose business was to manage the profession and form the policies for its future.

But the central, governing idea in Victor's Plan was not endorsed in this conference: that is, that moral education should be regarded as a subject in its own right, to be taught in classrooms and resourced as richly as any other major subject with syllabuses, learning materials and so on. Brian Ashley made it clear that the study group had had serious doubts about whether responsibility could be readily taught, and they rejected any suggestion that it might constitute a separate component of the curriculum. The concept of responsibility had implications for the total behaviour of the individual and must therefore be seen within the total social context of the individual. They concluded that the process of 'teaching' responsibility could only be effective if it led to 'a demonstrated capacity to engage in responsible behaviour'. This would involve decision taking, making choices between alternative forms of action. The schooling process must therefore develop real opportunities for the practice of decision making, not only in the pupil's personal affairs but also in areas which affect their social and educational development. The whole institutional life of the school must be engaged in the process of 'looking at where and when there were appropriate areas within the life of the institution in which possible decisions could be made, and should be made, by the pupils, and be seen by them to be relevant to their overall lives'.

So much of this is now part and parcel of the received wisdom in modern education that it is necessary to stress its novelty in 1981. What we recognise as 'democratic values' are now widely manifested in class, year and school councils, in giving pupils a measure of autonomy in curricular choice and in the provision of experience in community service programmes to exercise responsibility in a variety of forms; and in modern citizenship education programmes the principles we then embraced are well established. It must be admitted, however, that teachers have good reason to complain that these 'values education' activities are strictly subordinated to the drive for higher academic standards, greater proofs of accountability and all the pressures exhibited by the publication of league tables and performance records. Yet the growth of support for values education, citizenship education and the exercise of individual responsibility has continued. The Gordon Cook Foundation can fairly claim to have played a strong part in that process, and this conference, so long ago, helped to point the way.

It became clear to me, after the conference, that 'responsibility education' was not an adequate term for what we wanted schools to do. As Alex Sharp pointed out, to say that anyone is behaving 'irresponsibly' is formally incorrect: everyone is 'responsible' by virtue merely of being human. When we talk about a person failing to show responsibility, we must mean that they are failing to live up to our standards, but this is in fact a difference in value perspective, a difference in some shared acceptance of what is acceptable or permissible behaviour. In attempting to establish 'responsibility' we are trying to provide many individuals with a common pattern of values, attitudes and norms of behaviour. When government, in its Regulations, enjoins schools to develop 'reasonable and responsible social attitudes and relationships', to cultivate 'consideration for others' and to encourage the practice of 'good manners, good attitudes to work, initiative and self-reliance', there is an assumption that those in authority are possessed of a set of socially conforming, approved patterns of conduct which are universally valid and permanent. But in a modern, multicultural society it is not easy to set fixed standards of conduct for everyone without invading people's democratic rights as citizens or even harming their identity as persons. We must avoid the inculcation of moral rules which have been arrived at arbitrarily and irrationally.

We now know that young people should be taught to arrive at moral values which they can commit themselves to by rational means; we must devise procedures for working out what is the 'right' decision in any given circumstances. The task for the moral educator is to help students to develop 'moral intelligence', to find rational morality for themselves as against imbibing values drummed into them by authority figures. Of course it is our purpose that our students will adopt, or at least recognise that they ought to adopt, a code of values that conforms, more or less, with the values we as educators approve. We can of course make lists of value statements we see as desirable goals in our teaching, but the true outcomes we aim for must be the skills and attitudes that allow students to reach desirable values for themselves. Any list is bound to be inadequate, because values (expressed, say, as nominal groups) have all the ambiguity that inhabits language. It is much less useful to ask 'What values should we teach?' than to ask 'How can we teach our pupils to understand the meanings of expressed values?' or 'How can we teach our pupils to arrive at values?'

George Thomson, in his paper *Educating for Responsibility*, reviews some major research studies devoted to the development of moral maturity, both through cognitive processes – the growth of moral judgements – and affective processes–the growth of empathy, the experience of other people's emotional states. With regard to teaching, Thomson concludes that 'whether or not school can teach values is open to debate'. But he reiterates the view that 'schools have some influence' because the prevailing values, staff behaviour, rules of discipline and so on – the hidden curriculum or ethos of a school – will provide a source of role models and a sense of social and moral security. He quotes the American moral educator, Thomas Lickona: 'The problem with societal and individual efforts to optimise moral development, to paraphrase Chesterton, is not that they have been tried and found wanting, but that they have never been tried.'

As the 1980s progressed, more systematic efforts to devise methodologies for developing moral maturity were evolved, largely owing to the work of Kohlberg's associates and the Association for Moral Education (AME); and the Gordon Cook Foundation was able to contribute in some ways. In 1983, having been awarded a Commonwealth Fellowship by the Australian government, I was able to spend some months visiting Australian schools, delivering talks and conducting seminars on a range of educational topics. One of my interests was the many rewarding efforts being made to teach citizenship and values, and I wrote a paper for the Board of Trustees which proposed, among other things, that we should adopt the term 'values education' in place of 'education for citizenship and character development'. The new designation had several advantages. It was employed throughout the world and its general meaning was well understood. It widened our purposes to include social, aesthetic and environmental values, which had all figured in Victor's writings. It allied the Foundation to many other agencies with similar aims. Above all, perhaps, it was a portmanteau expression which was both suitably comprehensive and conveniently vague, allowing us to take an interest in a wider range of educational activities. Victor and our colleagues were happy to agree with the change; but Victor himself called our work Value Education to the end of his days. And to the end of his days he continued to try to defend the integrity of his own Plan – especially its central tenet, that explicit moral education should be given an acknowledged role in personal and social education.

Chapter Nine

The 1980s: progress

By 1980 Victor was sending kits, Handbooks and Log Books to more than a dozen primary and secondary schools in Aberdeen, and to several Lothian schools, mostly secondary, through the good offices of the Adviser in Guidance, Roy Dyer, and his colleague, Janette Fancey. This was a meagre return for all the hard work he had put in, but it kept him busy and every new school that agreed to help him brought him renewed hope. The kits comprised hundreds of items, expensively hand-typed and duplicated on equipment he had installed in dedicated rooms in Countesswells House. He had already decided that he would in due course enjoin his trustees to make use of the house as a centre for work on values education. The schools favoured kits dealing with social issues, such as 'Children Learn what they Live', a health education theme, with leaflets and booklets obtained from government-sponsored health education organisations; another popular kit was 'Abuse of Alcohol', which included topic worksheets, playlets, factsheets and a 16mm film called 'Dying of Thirst'. As might have been expected the materials from the official bodies were much more attractive and arresting than those produced by Victor's team. Some of this material now has the added interest that it was obviously Victor's own work. For example, teaching notes for a lesson on 'Care of School Property' includes the following:

> There are 1500 pupils at - - - - - -. If 1% of them (15) break a window costing £9.60 to replace each term, what is the value of windows destroyed in a year. £9.60 x 15 x 3 = £432.00. Collect suggestions on how this sum of money could be better used.

We can recognise Victor's hand: the absence of the question mark, the preoccupation with value for money, the naivety; on the face of it, sensible enough, but more likely to appeal to elderly business people than to young pupils. The publicity leaflet he sent out around this time has the same characteristic mixture of good intentions and artless ineffectiveness.

It is sad to reflect that while Victor and his associates were working hard to produce ineffectual teaching matter, the education system around them was abundant with approaches and courses which gave real evidence of the kind of education he had set his heart on developing. The Munn Committee's liberal and humane philosophy was being translated into new patterns of curriculum and teaching. Its companion body, the Dunning Committee, produced a reformed system of examinations and course assessment and proposed ingenious arrangements in timetabling to allow a flexibility in curriculum delivery which was unprecedented in British educational history. All over Scotland schools were designing courses specially adapted to appeal to their own pupils and give them new opportunities for learning and preparing for life. There was a vitality and commitment among teaching staff that kindled a new kind of confidence in their pupils. A number of official reports provided strong encouragement and guidance. After the Munn and Dunning reports came the Pack Report, *Truancy and Indiscipline in Schools in Scotland* (1977) which, despite its forbidding title, presented enlightened perspectives on how young people can be helped to live securely while studying. In 1980 a study, *Scottish Schools Councils*, by Macbeth, Mackenzie and Breckenbridge, opened up discussions about how schools should develop more democratic structures for decision making and policy forming. An important report, *An Education for Life and Work* (1983), proposed new approaches to the preparation of pupils for work and training. The Consultative Committee on the Curriculum (CCC) and its numerous subject groups produced reports on Guidance, Social Education, Religious Education, Contemporary Studies, Creative and Aesthetic Studies, Music, English Language and Literature; and the Committee on Primary Education (COPE) issued several studies of new approaches in primary school teaching. Nearly all of these reports had some bearing on the concerns which Victor touched upon in his Plan. Schools were, to a large extent, already moving towards the ideal situation he envisaged, when young people would be given an education in how to live morally and in the service of others.

Because I was actively involved in many of these curricular developments, being a member of the CCC and its governing Chairman's Committee, I was able to ensure that Victor received the reports. It was not so easy to give him advice as to how the Foundation should develop to take account of the national changes. Being engaged in the implementation of the new policies in a large region I was in a position to learn from the practical wisdom of teachers who worked at 'the chalk face'. But what was one to say to a man whose whole life was dedicated to a 'Plan' which – while not at serious odds with official policies – was essentially not suitable for adoption without fundamental and no doubt (to Victor) disastrous changes? At that time, in the early eighties, only two of his trustees knew much about education, and neither of us had the desire, or the time, or the vehemence, to confront Victor with the kind of unpalatable truths that would challenge all the work he was doing, and virtually force him into abdicating from his main purposes for living. There seemed to be only two strategies available to us: one was to keep him informed as far as possible with developments he could endorse and perhaps further by means of funding; and the other was to encourage him to try to achieve in his lifetime an object he had enjoined us to actualise after his death, the establishment of a Centre for Education in Values and Citizenship.

I had strong hopes that the publication of the CCC's report *Social Education in Scottish Schools* (1984) would further the first of these strategies. Its contents related in many ways to the work of the Gordon Cook Foundation. It described social education as being concerned 'with the development of those aspects of personality and intellect which allow a person to function effectively as a member of many groups, eg family, friendship, community, social and political groups . . .'; it went on to argue that social education 'is also concerned with the development of attitudes and feelings which enable [a young person] to form and maintain social relationships, to be adaptable to changing circumstances, to be conscious of the individual's responsibility towards the group and the group's responsibility towards the individual'. It emphasised that the school, especially the primary school, should be seen to share responsibility for social education with the home and the community. The values of the family will form the basis for attitudes to life which will probably remain central to the character and outlook of the individual. The school should collaborate actively with the parents to develop the knowledge and skills to enable young people to cope with the increasing demands of the wider community; it should actively encourage the acceptance of the right to hold different opinions, views or beliefs, and provide children with first-hand experience of relationships exemplifying appreciation of others, their feelings, views, needs and capacities. Most of these sentiments can be found in Victor's own writings in support of his Plan, albeit his language was more homespun and less fashionable.

One important dimension of educational thought exemplified in this and other reports from the CCC was an awareness of the multicultural and diversified character of British society. Victor could heartily agree with their assertion that 'children's beliefs, values and emotional stances in various areas of knowledge and behaviour spring from early origins' – he frequently made this point and devoted much more time and effort on primary and preschool work. But he was not sensitive to the argument that modern society represents a very wide range of attitudes, values and lifestyles that must be respected by teachers, and that they should 'develop a community perspective' and 'use all available avenues capable of leading to mutual understanding'. Had he grasped this whole-school, community-oriented perspective, Victor could well have radically altered his thinking in relation to education in values. But he was unable to abandon the simple beliefs and methodology he had founded his team's efforts upon, and because they seemed to share his outlook they continued to churn out their classroom materials without being able to fit them into the schools' cultural framework. In any case, the CCC's authors were too tentative in their approach for Victor's taste. Years before, when HMI W. J. H. Earl had tried to comfort Victor with a mention of the interest being engendered in Scotland following the publication of the Millar Report, Victor had said, 'There is a tremendous vagueness yet.' He would certainly want to say the same of the CCC's reports. The writers were all experienced educators with sufficient practical experience to be realistic about what was feasible for everyday schooling. They were clear about their own intentions: they wanted schools to initiate an education in values which would be central to the life of the school and the community, but they were aware that this would require careful planning and development. They were conscious that schools ought to provide pupils with an understanding of, and commitment to, the recognised values of the society they served, and they took it for granted that these values could readily be described and elaborated; but they were not at all sure that schools would be free to teach them without opposition: 'Ideally', said the authors of the social education report, 'the school, the family and the wider community will share the same values and attitudes, but schools cannot take that for granted. Indeed, the school may not be able to take for granted that the values which it as an organisation embodies are shared by society in its widest sense any longer at all.' The values the CCC proposed for teaching (as listed in the Munn Report) were 'the capacity to show concern for others, to cooperate, to be rational, to respect evidence, to work hard, to be resourceful and to find satisfaction in learning'. The social education report is explicit in its insistence that it is a value-laden activity: 'the values themselves are often, quite intentionally, the main focus of teaching and learning.' It acknowledges that 'an important aim of social education is to develop values broadly in harmony with those cherished by society as a whole'. 'Clearly', it goes on, 'there is agreement, at the most fundamental level, on the values which underpin our way of life.' It quotes the report of the Secretary of State's project on Education for the Industrial Society, *An Education for Life and Work*. Referring to the seminal report of 1947 on Secondary Education, the authors (of whom I was one) sum up the case for education in values:

> An education for the whole person must also promote what a distin-guished education report called the democratic virtues, which it listed as 'tolerance, respect for reason and persuasion, hatred of cruelty and oppression, the willingness to surrender sectional privileges in the general interest and to sacrifice personal leisure in the common service, and, not least, an international temper of sympathy and understanding.'

Under Victor Cook's leadership the Gordon Cook Foundation really stood for these values, but it would add what might be called the 'personal values' of compassion, fairness and honesty. It was frustrating to realise that Victor was unable to connect fruitfully with those in the education system who basically shared his aspirations. His influence would have been powerful: he firmly believed that education should be instrumental in securing social cohesion and prosperity, but he also, more emphatically, believed that it should teach the young to enjoy the good life of a decent individual.

Another source of evidence to demonstrate the great activity and optimism of the early years of the 1980s, especially in Scotland, can be seen in a book, *Educating for Tomorrow*, published in 1984 for Lothian Region Education Department. The book presented a 'Lothian perspec-tive', expressing the experiences, values and judgements of a representative range of senior staff. As W. D. C. Semple, the enlightened Director of Education, wrote in his foreword, the book set out to give the readers, in particular the rate-payers, the elected members, the staff of the region, the teachers, parents, and the general public, a picture of education in a large Scottish region, to 'highlight problems and discuss possible solu-tions'. He claimed, with good reason, that the picture presented was representative of Scottish education at its best. The authors comprised nine advisers, seven head teachers, four depute heads, two principals of further education colleges, the head of special educational services, the regional careers officer and the regional community education officer. As Chief Adviser I edited the book with the assistance of Bruce Wallace, regional adviser in Religious Education. In my Introduction I wrote:

> The school today tries to cater for three 'domains' of learning: the

cognitive, which has to do with knowledge and intellectual skills; the aesthetic, which concerns cultural and artistic development; and the affective, which has to do with personality, character, attitudes, self-concepts, ideals and all the qualities our society conceives as essential for a well-rounded, happy and useful existence.

I added that schools were often criticised for neglecting to provide adequate training for the personal development of pupils. Bruce Wallace discussed the rationale for personal development in schools. In arguing for more commitment to social and personal development – allowing young people to experiment in their personal development through the use of role-play, games and simulations and to help them to personalise insights into the human condition he pleaded for more attention to how pupils can act purposefully within a moral framework. Even in what he called 'our presently chilly economic clime' the cost of maturing experiences – in such activities as Drama and Outdoor Education and the arts – should be seen to be worth bearing. As the adviser in Religious Education he was able to claim that the subject could provide a focus for all disparate contributions to personal development; questions about the nature, meaning, value and purpose of life are central to RE, where teachers can encourage in pupils the development of a comprehensive philosophy of the person. I was very much struck with this argument, and took it up in later years with a number of RE specialists. My position was that Victor was quite right in asserting that moral education should be provided independently of religious education, but I could see no reason why teachers of religious education should not take a leading role in the whole-school programme of moral and social education. Their education and training surely fitted them for that. The Christian ethic was, after all, the most widely accepted moral code in our society, and while there was of course ample justification for the teaching of doctrinal principles in any acknowledged faith – that was for the wider community to deal with – teachers of RE could wear the 'other hat'. Of course that role could well be taken up by any other teacher.

Victor Cook was never clear in his mind about the relationship between religious and moral education. He frequently reminded people that his plan for the dedicated teaching of morality should be 'complementary' to religious education, but he never seems to have attempted to elaborate the notion. He was not himself a devout Christian, though he supported the kirk and respected the role of religion in the lives of people and its entitlement to a central place in education. Although he was never in a position to involve himself with curriculum planning he frequently participated in discussions with RE specialists about the aims and procedures of moral education. He was delighted when, later in the decade, a strong lead was taken in values education by Catholic schools.

Bruce Wallace's reference to the 'chilly economic clime' which confronted British education at that time pointed to the policy of retrenchment which began with the recession of the mid-seventies and sharply increased with the advent of the Thatcher government in 1979.

The demographic and economic changes which increased the number of pupils seeking school certificates also motivated the government to effect savings elsewhere, and this combined with a new emphasis on higher performance in the conventional academic subjects to threaten the curriculum areas devoted to affective development. Cash limits were imposed on public spending from 1976 onwards. In the early eighties cuts in the rate support grant forced education authorities to make stringent savings, and in the mid-eighties rate-capping exacerbated their plight. Government interventions to improve educational standards continued, but these increasingly took the form of programmes intended to increase the nation's economic efficiency: TVEI (Technical and Vocational Education Initiative) and the YTS (Youth Training Scheme), the new Training Initiative and the Action Plan for 16- to 18-year-olds – which encouraged attendance at further education colleges for vocational courses – were all designed to push the curricula towards more vocational education and specialised training for industry and commerce. Paradoxically, the 1980s saw a great flourishing of educational innovation and experimentation alongside an increasingly bitter struggle between educational practitioners and government policy makers. Central government's dilemma was that they needed to improve the educational process for important economic reasons and at the same time reduce expenditure on it. Teachers became frustrated by continual pressures for more effective performance and reduced costs. Managerialism was imported from the business world to devise the means for greater accountability, more stringent supervision and more methodical measurements of performance. There was also a greater assertiveness in political rhetoric: teachers were subjected to criticisms that they ought to work harder, that they were already overpaid as a result of generous settlements in the sixties and seventies, and that they needed to adopt more realistic – utilitarian – notions of their duties and their roles in preparing young people for life and work.

Teachers felt that they were made scapegoats for the economic ineffi-
ciency of government, that their salary levels had been deliberately
allowed to decline since the seventies. The teaching unions demanded an
independent pay review, but this was directly contrary to government
policy. In 1984 the Scottish teachers began an industrial action which lasted
for two years, badly damaging various curriculum development projects
and threatening to disrupt the national examinations. Even after a settle-
ment in 1986 there was a residue of resentment among teachers which
compelled government officers to effect change, such as the implementation of the Munn Report, by using inspectors and seconded staff as
central agents. A change had come over education throughout the United
Kingdom: teachers were suspicious of government policies, reluctant to
do more than their statutory duties, and most of the life of the school
dependent on voluntary effort suffered decline.

In Aberdeen, Victor felt the change: he was less welcome in the schools;
fewer teachers wanted to use his material. As his trustees were now
pointing out, his approaches were failing to keep pace with the changes in
the current of professional opinion. But these frustrations were to some
extent ameliorated by renewed vigour among the trustees themselves.
The death of Sydney Davidson and Bertram Tawse brought in two new
trustees in 1982: the Reverend Derek Henderson and Sir Maitland Mackie.
Derek was Victor's parish minister; he was a man of congenial tempera-
ment and very sympathetic to the purposes of the Foundation. Although
he was not knowledgeable about modern education he had had business
experience and he was particularly interested in youth movements and
education that encouraged enterprise in the young. Maitland Mackie was
a prominent north-east farmer, a shrewd businessman, a hearty and clever
speaker; he had a keen interest in the provision of education, having been
for many years the convener of Aberdeenshire Education Committee.
Both were eager to help the Foundation to prosper and develop, and they
were eager to listen to the advice of the professional educationists. They
were useful in the business aspects of our responsibilities as trustees
and they were able to exert a benign influence on their old friend Victor.

In 1985 the Foundation enjoyed a decisive stroke of good fortune
with the involvement of B. J. (Bart) McGettrick, principal of St Andrew's
College of Education, Glasgow, a leading figure in the Scottish Catholic
Church and a powerful presence in Scottish education. Here is Bart's
own account of his introduction to Victor Cook and the Gordon Cook
Foundation:

Reflections from B. J. McGettrick on Early Associations with Victor Cook

In the middle part of the 1960s there was a significant democratisation process that influenced the whole of society. It was made manifest in pop music through the Beatles; it was demonstrated in film and theatre by many 'liberal' events and productions; and no aspect of society was immune from the effects of this significant social change. In the Catholic Church there was a period of significant reflection through the Second Vatican Council.

The first publication of the Second Vatican Council of the Church was a document on education. Twenty years after its publication there was a meeting of educationists invited from across the world to come to Rome to reflect on that document and to consider how it had an impact on values and ideals in education. One of the people invited was a major figure in education in India – Sister Pia Nazareth. I was also present at this event. I had seen Sister Pia at the conference but there had been no time to engage in conversation.

Just as the conference finished I got on the Number 40 bus from the Vatican en route to the station. Characteristically this bus was full . . . and it is notorious for pickpockets. At the next stop Sister Pia Nazareth got on the same bus and there were no seats left. I offered my seat to Sister Pia who then engaged me in a conversation asking if I was from England. I indicated that I was from Scotland and, to my astonishment, she said, 'Oh! Well you must know Victor Cook and Bill Gatherer!' I indicated that I knew Bill Gatherer but did not know Victor Cook. Sister Pia then suggested that I should be in touch with Bill and get to know Victor Cook.

On my return to Scotland I did get in touch with Bill and through him I got in touch with Victor Cook. My first meeting with Victor was an invitation to lunch in Braemar. He invited me on a Sunday after-noon to meet him at a hotel in Braemar and then to travel with him to Aberdeen.

My recollection of lunch in Braemar was to meet Victor around mid-day. He arrived from Aberdeen in a very large, heavy black car. He seemed to be dressed in traditional tweeds for a Sunday afternoon drive. Following lunch Victor suggested that we travel to Balmoral where he would show me the estates which were part of his childhood. That was a memorable journey!

Victor led me from Braemar to Balmoral at a speed which didn't allow me to move much beyond second gear in a car. After about a mile I noticed we had an extremely long tail of traffic which increased in length and frustration on the road between Braemar and Balmoral. I doubt if Victor noticed. Having reached Balmoral we stopped at a gate which read 'Royal Estates: Strictly No Entry'. Victor got out of his car, opened the gates, drove through the gates and ushered me to follow him. Having closed the gates behind us he then took off at a speed which meant that I was in fourth gear even going around hairpin bends. There was dust everywhere and Victor showed me the Balmoral Estates.

That night I spent a night of fitful sleeping in Countesswells House in Aberdeen. The roof was open to the stars and the bird life clearly enjoyed the comfort which this provided.

I shared many reflections with Victor during that visit and communication became more frequent. I also reflected on some of the development that arose from Sister Pia in India and began to develop an interest in Values Education and I was struck by the twin context that Victor brought to considering value in education. On the one hand he was in touch with significant figures at a global level (eg Presidents of the United States, Gorbachev, leading figures in education in India, etc); and on the other hand he was passionate about the work of children in schools in Aberdeen. He operated in these two dramatically different contexts. In my discussions with him I often reflected that most people operate in some middle ground and that he should be encouraged to think about national groups in Scotland.

Subsequently in 1988 I was invited to become a Trustee of the Gordon Cook Foundation. I attended my first meeting in the Station Hotel in Aberdeen – recalling that it was preceded by 'a modest lunch' which in Aberdonian terms was indeed modest!

My initial reaction as a Trustee was to welcome this opportunity while being rather concerned with the uncertain strategies and plans of the Foundation. The openness and willingness to invest in the contemporary agencies for development soon provided the comfort that the Foundation would be a significant contributor to developing values and citizenship in education in Scotland and beyond.

In 1986 I reported to the board of trustees that I had met Bart McGettrick to inform him about the Foundation and recommended that Victor and he should meet. Very soon afterwards St Andrew's College was actively involved in our work. Bart and I had agreed that a seminar might be held for his staff and others interested, and this occurred in the following year. A member of Bart's staff, Stephen Joyce, was appointed coordinator of the new values education programme. Stephen proved to be a man after Victor's own heart: he entered wholeheartedly into Victor's world-view, sharing his simple commitment to what Victor had long called 'the abiding truths', and striving to persuade teachers to make use of the prepared materials. But he brought a new dimension of pedagogic skill to the work, and soon had a number of primary schools in Glasgow and the surrounding district working at 'themes' based on given values and illustrated by stories and projects. Soon Victor and Stephen were in constant touch, meeting and planning devices to deepen teachers' interest. They conducted an essay competition for student teachers, offering attractive money prizes; and they visited schools together, to Victor's great delight and enlightenment. Arrangements were begun to initiate an optional course in Values Education as part of the BEd degree. To help with resources Victor had large sections of E. B. Castle's book, *The Teacher*, reprinted and issued gratis.

It is probably true to say that acquaintanceship with the Gordon Cook Foundation gave Bart McGettrick a new interest in what he called 'educating the whole person'. He expressed his thoughts in a preface he wrote for a document issued by the college entitled *Citizenship and Values Education – Pilot Project 1987–1988*:

Fashions in education change, just as fashions in society change. An international trend as we approach the end of the twentieth century is the concern for the values we hold and how these are influenced by education. The purpose of education as making people – children and adults – more suited for life, demands that we pay attention to those essential values.

For a large part of this century the focus of educational endeavour has been on the curriculum, and, quite properly, in improving curricular provision in our schools. Education has its influence beyond the curriculum, in the ways people interact with each other, in the values we demonstrate by our actions, and by our internal reflections and growth. These values, often springing from the most intimate cradles of our lives – our homes, families and friends – cannot be neglected or we do not take responsibility for tomorrow's world. The world of tomorrow is the product of yesterday's society and today's values.

It is encouraging for those of us involved in formal education to recognise the deeply held commitment of others to the real qualities of education – the education of values. The Gordon Cook Foundation represents in Scotland that commitment and concern for the formation of values of young people. Through the labours and interest of Victor Cook and his Trustees of the Foundation there is a motivation to form people with informed values so that civilization lives and thrives in the hearts of men.

It is this vision which St Andrew's College understands to be the shared commitment of the Foundation and the College, and it is a shared vision which we jointly wish to provide in the interests of citizenship for tomorrow's world.

Although it was issued by the college, bearing its coat of arms alongside a logo Victor had designed, the report is clearly the work of Victor himself and Stephen Joyce. It presented Victor's Plan as a 'detailed method of teaching explicitly Value Education for character or personal development along with Social and Health Studies as a systematised discipline to supplement existing practice and complementary to religious education'. Victor's introductory piece, titled 'THE NEED', is a familiar recital of his personal rationale, but it displays an improved understanding and a rather more polished style which suggests that Stephen had a hand in its composition; yet it represents Victor's deepfelt outlook in a fresh manner:

THE NEED

The future of any society is determined by the quality of its youth, who in turn are profoundly influenced by upbringing, the principal influences being the home, school, religion and leisure activities. The influence of the parents is the most profound and lasting, but it is difficult to influence parents. A means of obtaining their co-operation is suggested.

How to instil the basic values is the burning question today. To know what they are – honesty, kindliness, courage and the like, is not sufficient but the teaching can show how utterly basic they are to society.

The pioneer psychologist, Professor William McDougall, maintained 'Men of all ages and of the most diverse creeds and civilisations are pretty well agreed as to what is good and what is bad conduct and character, such differences as obtain being merely matters of emphasis on this or that quality.'

These are the 'eternal verities' that do not change with the changing times.

Over a wide area of educational thinking the subject is receiving much attention, but there seems now to be needed a systematic but flexible approach to personal development, open minded as to the relationship of moral to religious education.

Many feel that now is the time for new ventures in this field involving not only teachers and children but parents and others. It is only in schools that all children are available for teaching by trained staff. Improvement could be possible by laying special emphasis on character development particularly in the early years when the foundations are laid at home and at primary school. It has been stated from earliest times and this aspect of education is of paramount importance. Society renews itself through its schools and it is here that the basic virtues should be acquired as effectively as the foundations of academic knowledge as expressed by so many educators today.

Under the present conditions the guidance of the rising generation formerly given in the home is now changing to dependence more on the school.

It is urged that every possible action be taken in relation to this vital matter.

The report contains material for college students prepared by Joyce: Points for Discussion, Assignments, examination questions and an invitation to write for an essay competition with prizes of '£100, £50, £30 and various sums for others depending on submissions'. Two senior members of the college staff were named as assessors. Other materials were inserted from Victor's cottage-industry publications: the Objectives (with 'Values' added), the Code of Behaviour, descriptions of the Topics, Log Books and Handbooks, and pious quotations from Henry Drummond's book – so greatly admired by Victor – *The Greatest Thing in the World*. There is also an essay, called 'Maturity Analysed' by one of Sister Pia Nazareth's students (the winning entry for a competition funded by Victor) and taken from Sister Pia's book, *A Child's World of Values*. On the whole, it was a distinct improvement on Victor's early efforts, but it is easy to imagine the feelings of slight embarrassment and scepticism among some of the highly professional educationists on the staff. I can testify myself, however, that Victor was always treated with great respect and courtesy by his new-found colleagues in the college.

The effect on Victor of this new relationship cannot be exaggerated. It gave him renewed hope that his Plan might be reaching the goal of acceptance; it gave him new ideas and new understandings of how education progressed; above all it gave him new friendships and new allies. I believe that it had a beneficent effect on his personal health.

Chapter Ten

Triumphs and anxieties

The accession of Bart McGettrick to the Foundation – a most important development, Victor called it – greatly increased our credibility in Scotland. We lost no time in making use of Bart's alliance: at a trustees' meeting soon after the 1987 seminar at St Andrew's College I proposed the election of Bart to the board. By now the board had become stronger and more efficient. David Levie, senior partner in Burnett and Reid, the law firm which acted for us (he was Maitland Mackie's son-in-law) replaced Farquhar MacRitchie as secretary; henceforth the minutes of meetings, which Victor had always written himself – rather selectively, it has to be said – were produced formally and in detail. In September 1988 Bart joined a trustees' meeting and was appointed to the board.

The financial strength of the Foundation was growing steadily, though Victor was always chary of encouraging expenditure; when I asked how much income could safely be spent on educational development, he warned us, as he often did, that while the portfolio valued had increased (by five times) this meant that the capital today was not a great deal more than the 'real value' of the original £100,000 'taking into account inflation'. He was evasive in answer to my question: 'it was difficult', the minutes recorded him saying, 'to ascertain this figure as it depended on the rate of inflation, the growth of investments and the policy of the Foundation regarding any provision for further development.' In the old days the trustees would have let this kind of answer suffice, but now we persisted. There was little point in planning further development if we had no exact knowledge of how much we could spend. Sir Maitland, who had proved a shrewd and constructive trustee though he knew very little about the educational issues, said that the Foundation now had an opening to spend its money usefully; the income for the year was approximately £41,000, and consequently £38,000 could safely be spent – 'and growth would come anyway'. Victor said that growth was only speculative. Jack Marshall 'stressed that more should be spent on education rather than investment'.

We were gravely discussing a proposal that had arisen during the spring of 1988: in 1987 we had discussed the possibility of setting up a Gordon

Cook Foundation Centre for Values Education, and now this idea had become a genuine intention to approach the SED to offer a donation towards the establishment of a national centre. I had begun discussions with former colleagues in the SED and with an old friend, David McNicoll, Chief Executive of what was now called the Scottish Consultative Council – the old CCC had been 'privatised' by the Conservative minister Michael Forsyth, in the sense that it had a board of directors, including persons from the world of business, and was in some degree independent of the SED, though the government remained its only funder. At my suggestion Victor wrote to Forsyth on 7 July about the proposal, and received a reply on 29 July giving, as Victor reported, 'unqualified support on the work of the Foundation stating "this is exactly the sort of development that we want to see in education at the present time"'. He added that 'he had met Mr Forsyth at a South Aberdeen Conservative meeting and handed to him a copy of Summary of Plan, a Note on International Relations, copy of Pilot Project at St Andrew's College of Education and a Note on three points to consider'. What Forsyth made of this is not known; no doubt he merely handed the papers over to an official, but it was sufficient that he let it be known that he wanted something done.

In October a meeting was held in New St Andrew's House to discuss the idea. To Victor, the overriding purpose of a Centre would be to make it easier to implement his Plan, but his trustees saw wider and more practical advantages. At the trustees' meeting in September, Bart spoke at some length about his own perspectives on the Foundation's work. Referring to the three projects we had now agreed to pursue – Victor's own work at Countesswells House, our work with St Andrew's College, and our approach to the SED – he suggested that our involvement in the curriculum 'would be achieved as a result of the Foundation's continued involvement with the SCCC.' He said the Foundation 'would be more influential if it indicated to the SED that it had a vision of the way in which the objects of the Foundation would be put into practice, setting out the financial and personal implications'. He proposed that a four-year plan should be drawn up coordinating the different areas and ensuring that the funding would be used efficiently and effectively.

There can be no doubt that Victor felt some anxiety about the direction events were taking. But he had agreed to go ahead. Soon after the trustees' meeting in September he wrote to the SED official responsible, J. W. L. Lonie, to say that he looked forward to the meeting and had, 'rather hurriedly', prepared some materials to be tabled: a Memorandum on a Values Education Centre, with an Appendix giving the 'Background' to the GCF, and he included a copy of the Memorandum he and his allies had submitted to the Schools Council in June 1971 – one of Victor's most satisfying achievements. It was not vanity that actuated him to bring up his past success in bringing about development. This was a manoeuvre in defence of his Plan: he wanted the SED officials to understand that he had experience in planning educational change; he was making sure that they were aware that it was his intentions, and his money, that needed to be at the heart of discussions. Pleased as he was to have new allies like Bart McGettrick, he was anxious lest the basic purposes of his own campaign might be dissipated in a flurry of officialese and bland revisions of his ideas so that the proffered funds would merely support work they were doing already.

His Memorandum began with the simple declaration that 'the Trustees of the Gordon Cook Foundation would like to see established a Values Education Centre in Scotland to promote the teaching of basic values in schools.' He then offered a 'statement' of what is meant by 'basic values'. This, however, was no more than the old familiar quotation from McDougall that 'men of all ages' are 'pretty well agreed' as to 'what is good and what bad in conduct and character'. Neither McDougall nor Victor Cook ever embarked upon a consideration of values as psychological dispositions or moral principles; McDougall was concerned with behaviour as manifestations of instincts, and Victor always assumed that values were 'eternal verities' that can be taught by precept and illustration. Time and again, his friends thought that we were succeeding in making him understand the need for research into the nature of values and values education, only to find him reverting to his old mentors. Yet his faith in simple universal values is widely held today.

Here he was again quoting from another old favourite, W. D. Wall, to the effect that 'the adolescent' needs to have a philosophic or religious self founded on a simple set of values and standards capable of interpreting life, of directing discussions and determining behaviour. This paragraph ends with another declaration: 'It would be the objectives of the Centre to promote such values.' Significantly, the Memorandum refers to the reports on Social Education (see below) and repeats the 'working definition': 'social education in schools should be concerned with personal and social issues which are relevant to young people . . .' and 'should be concerned with "feeling" and "doing" as well as knowing, and should seek to promote the active involvement of pupils in the process of learning'. Since Victor wrote this Memorandum himself, it can be taken to represent his own position: he was willing to fund a Values Education Centre, and he was content that it should work in conformity with 'the work already carried out by the Scottish Education Department on Values Education in the various reports over many years'; but he also claimed that the objectives and methods of the work carried out by his own Foundation complied with the definition given in the Social Education reports, and he wanted 'further work' to include 'the development and application' of his own endeavours in the field. He was well aware that a national centre could achieve more than he himself ever could:

> For over 18 years I have done my utmost to further the Objectives of the Foundation. Only now with the introduction to a Teacher Training College have we obtained what we sought so long, but I realise that our Foundation, or any private such institution, could never achieve the results of a Centre part of the Scottish Education Department with its stamp of Authority, influence and resources.

Victor had suggested to Michael Forsyth that the centre might be called the Gordon Cook Centre, but he now felt that that would be 'much less satisfactory': 'the new proposal is that the Values Education Centre would be under the aegis of the Scottish Education Department'. And he added, 'If this proposal is agreed I will be prepared to give a Grant, from my personal means, separate from the Foundation to enable a start to be made as soon as possible.' The income from the grant could be supplemented by 'indirect support from my home at Aberdeen and St Andrew's College of Education.' His decision to provide the grant from his own purse stemmed from the discussion we had had at the September trustees' meeting, when we discussed finance: he had decided, he told me, that the Foundation could not afford to fund a national centre and at the same time carry on with our other two projects, his own work and that at St Andrew's College. Another reason was that he was anxious to see the Centre up and running as soon as possible – in his innocence he thought, understandably, that having got the money they could go ahead without further ado. He soon learned, of course, that further ado was a normal condition with government-funded quangos. On the evening after our meeting with the SED he phoned me to say that he had been doing some sums on the train home, and he had decided that our grant of £100,000 was not enough to meet the costs of maintaining a centre and contribute to the cost of the salary of a development officer; so he had decided to double it. Would I please inform the SED people that the grant would now be £200,000.

The Memorandum was passed to the Chief Executive of the SCCC, David McNicoll, and he lost no time in consulting his Council and drafting an Agreement. Although Victor had concluded the transaction without formal reference to his board of trustees (though he no doubt communicated with others as well as myself by telephone) the Agreement was drawn up legally as between the Trustees of the GCF and the SCCC, thus ensuring that there could be continuity of supervision on our part and that it could be changed or modified or cancelled at any time in the future; if either party should wish to withdraw from the agreement the balance of the grant would revert to the Foundation.

It was a cleverly written and structured document. The SCCC staff entertained some reservations about the intentions of the GCF, and McNicoll had some difficulty in persuading some of the members of his Council to agree that the grant should be accepted. The offer of course was very attractive: at that time £200,000 was a very large sum and the arrangement pleased the minister. But there were doubts as to what the GCF was actually wanting the SCCC to do. Victor's Memorandum was not very helpful in elucidating our intentions. Moreover they were getting conflicting impressions from different people: Bart was a member of the SCCC, and he was able to reassure his colleagues that we were not following some sinister agenda of our own; and David McNicoll and I were former colleagues and still good friends, so he was able to get information from me informally and frankly; and in his frequent meetings with Victor during this period he formed a very favourable impression of his honesty and simple integrity. He was left with no illusions about Victor's determination that values education should have a strong element of direct teaching of moral and social values, but he understood that the trustees concerned were happy with the views of the official working parties which had all decided that moral education must be a whole-school responsibility. In my view that did not preclude the need for research and reflection on the nature of values and how they might best be assimilated by pupils in structured learning.

The Agreement explicitly accepted that its purpose was to 'ensure continuity' of the objectives of the GCF 'programme applied in schools to foster Values Education', the grant being intended to assist the SCCC 'to promote and apply the principles of Values and Citizenship in Education within the curriculum of schools in Scotland'. Accordingly a Values Education Centre would be established by the SCCC in conjunction with the GCF. 'Values in education', it said, 'are broadly described as commonly admired human values, attitudes and modes of behaviour,' and Citizenship as 'the attributes, knowledge and social skills which enable young persons to develop into active and useful members of the community in which they live'. The document asserts that these descriptions are 'contiguous' with stated positions taken and published by the GCF and by the SCCC. This rather nebulous account is followed by a pledge to 'promote and apply the principles of Values and Citizenship in Education' within 'ongoing curriculum development programmes with resources agreed by the Secretary of State for Scotland'. The concept of values in education would be examined by a Review and Development Group. The Council would establish within its premises a Centre (or centres) where relevant published and unpublished materials would be held. The reference to 'a Centre (or centres)' was made because the SCCC had at that time three centres, in Glasgow, Edinburgh and Dundee, and staff were reluctant to comply with the proposal that they should be amalgamated into one.

We had stipulated that the grant be invested and the income devoted to maintaining the centre and meeting the cost of a development officer dedicated to values education. The SCCC quibbled about that and the Agreement committed them only to employ a part-time director, but they agreed to assign other staff to aspects of the work. They undertook to submit an annual report to the GCF. Despite some reservations, Victor signed the Agreement along with David McNicoll on 22 December 1988.

Victor was certainly now confident that his long campaign was beginning to bear fruit. For years he had resisted his trustees' attempts to get him to publish his writings properly, to be interviewed on television or to have a film made about his work, but in April 1989 he agreed to be interviewed by Calum MacDonald of the Aberdeen *Press and Journal*. Excerpts from the article reveal a lively personality and a serious, reflective mind:

In 1967 Mr Cook had meetings with Lord Reith the BBC's first Director General when both shared the view that the root of many troubles affecting young people of the day lay largely with the influences on the child's mind during the first five years at home and then at the primary school. These meetings were the main inspirations for a major new initiative.

Lord Reith then asked Mr Cook to draw up a blueprint for change and it was formulated in 1967. So was born the Scottish version of 'Values Education' which had already been tried successfully in other parts of the world.

Following the death of his father, Mr Cook took the helm at the

Aberdeen Engineering firm Barry, Henry and Cook. In 1973 he sold his majority shareholding to Seaforth Maritime, an oil related company.

This enabled Mr Cook to invest a substantial sum in establishing the Gordon Cook Foundation, formally set up in 1974, with a name reflecting the surname of both his parents; the foundation adopted a clear Charter of objectives and values. Broadly stated, these centred on the need for young people to be brought to maturity through a well-rounded education which stresses the importance of character development.

Now a sprightly 91 Mr Cook says: 'At one time, values were considered the province of the home and children learned them from their parents, but we realise today that the schools often have to take that responsibility.'

Mr Cook believes in working closely with the educational establishment, and his project has been blessed by many top figures in the field.

The Foundation Trustees – Sir Maitland Mackie, former Lord Lieutenant of Aberdeenshire; Dr W. A. Gatherer, former Chief Education Adviser to Lothian Region; Mr John Marshall a retired Head Teacher; Mr B. J. McGettrick, Principal, St Andrew's College of Education; Inverness-based the Rev. Roderick Henderson and former RGIT Principal Dr Peter Clarke – helped ensure the credibility of his aims.

The past 15 years have been spent on behind-the-scenes activity. A number of teachers – either retired or with young children who restrict the time they can spend in the classroom – have worked part-time on ready-made material for use in values education. There is no attempt at uniformity of approach, and teachers are encouraged on a voluntary basis to try out the material and adapt it to their own needs and style.

Mr Cook admits: 'It's easy to lay down rules and objectives, but the difficulty is to get them implemented and accepted naturally'.

The Foundation has also, in recent years, promoted the good citizenship ideal through awards to pupils.

A document which dropped through his letterbox on the morning of our interview had given him considerable pleasure. The Scottish Education Department's latest working paper on the primary curriculum renewed his hope that values education could become part of mainstream teaching. The paper includes the recommendation: 'Moral Education should be developed implicitly and explicitly in every school. Opportunities for the development of moral values are present, and should be taken, in virtually every aspect of the curriculum. By the establishment of a caring atmosphere and by emphasis on good personal relationships, the ethos of the school will be an important element in developing appropriate moral values and a sense of collective and individual responsibility'.

The heightened involvement which parents are about to be granted in school management will surely strengthen the partnership between home and classroom. It is hard to imagine that fundamental values of honesty, kindness, respect and love will be omitted from the dialogue.

Mr Cook is clear: 'Values should be taught implicitly and explicitly in schools'. As H. G. Wells said, 'it is now a race between that kind of education and disaster'. And as Mr Gorbachev said to the United Nations last December, 'the primacy should be on these universal human values that everybody accepts'.

I put it to this well-read, highly-articulate bachelor that the absence of children or grandchildren from his life must make him slightly sad. The answer was a philosophical acceptance of his lot, and the admission that his fascination for this subject – and his other love, preventative health care, kept him fully occupied.

There is a well-disguised beam of delight on his face when he says: 'One of the Trustees told me the other day "what you were advocating 20 years ago is all coming to the surface now"'.

Victor was now aware that his health was precarious. His doctors had noted an aortic aneurysm and judged that surgery would be dangerous and probably fatal. He told his friends quite cheerfully that 'he could go at any minute, but he intended to work away as usual'. He did, however, approach Dr Peter Clarke and asked for his help. Dr Clarke contacted Helen Innes, newly retired from the College of Commerce, and arranged for her to assist Victor at Countesswells House. This arrangement worked very well: she had soon organised his chaotic office and his correspondence, and she also 'mothered' him, seeing that he ate and dressed properly. During 1989 Peter often visited Victor and gave him such advice as he could about his work, his health and his lifestyle. Peter had long been a fellow member of the Aberdeen Business and Professional Club, and while he knew little about the Foundation and its purposes he proved to be a real strength to Victor. Dr Peter Clarke CBE was an eminent figure in Scottish higher education: he had been a university lecturer, Vice Principal of Huddersfield Technical College, and currently he was Principal of Robert Gordon Institute of Technology (now the Robert Gordon University). He was also chairman of the Scottish Vocational Education Council (SCOTVEC), the most influential body concerned with vocational education and training in Scotland. At the meeting of the

GCF trustees on 4 January 1989 he was elected a trustee, and thereafter proved to be a strong and wise proponent of our endeavours.

At our meeting of 31 October 1989 we elected two more trustees, both excellent acquisitions to our strength. Two years earlier I had recommended to Victor that he should make contact with David Adams, Principal of the Northern College of Education in Aberdeen. Long before, Victor had approached the then principal, David's predecessor, James Scotland, but did not get a warm welcome and came away dispirited and convinced (wrongly) that he had made another enemy. His meeting with David Adams was quite different: he was listened to courteously, enjoyed a fruitful discussion, and later reported to the trustees that Mr Adams had favourably received his request for support. David brought an important degree of authority and prestige to the Foundation. We now had three trustees who represented the Scottish educational establishment at its best, and Jack Marshall and I were delighted to have their collegial friendship and guidance. At the same meeting we appointed Charles Skene OBE to the board. Charles was another prize for us. A highly successful businessman, he was also an authority on the subjects of enterprise education and entrepreneurship. Since 1986 he had been leading and largely funding the Skene Awards, a scheme for encouraging an enterprising culture in schools by helping them to set up 'mini-businesses' staffed and managed by pupils. Charles was also active in promoting more adventurous business ventures in Scotland. With his recruitment we now had a new set of values to consider, and a new source of energy: in a country where it was crucial to bring up generations of men and women who could be economically productive, it was right that a Foundation devoted to education for citizenship and character should encourage the young to be enterprising. With Derek Henderson, Maitland Mackie, Charles Skene and of course Victor himself, we now had a reservoir of business experience and knowledge, and with Bart McGettrick, Peter Clarke, David Adams, Jack Marshall and myself we had a balancing store of knowledge and experience in the field of education. It was a highly productive mixture, and we had many stimulating, provocative and entertaining arguments over many years. Victor could now congratulate himself that his Foundation, so long little known and so often slighted, could now address the educational and political world with confidence and the expectation to be heard with respect.

He was not entirely satisfied, however, with the way the SCCC was fulfilling its promises. They were not, apparently, prepared to set up a national centre of the kind we had envisaged; rather they undertook to distribute work on 'values in education' over their three existing centres, with a 'centre' in their Dundee premises for books and documents – a small and badly equipped room, Victor thought. They had undertaken to 'promote' education in values and citizenship in agreement with the GCF, but they were vague, and possibly even disingenuous, about using Victor's own hard-won materials and methods. Victor's response to these suspicions was, characteristically, to conduct a campaign of letters and phone-calls to everyone he considered to be a decision maker. At first his main target was Jim Lonie of the SED; soon his attention was concentrated on David McNicoll, the chief executive of the SCCC. For a few years now Victor had been able to use a telephone with sound amplification; so he was on equal terms on the phone, whereas his deafness had been a real disadvantage in ordinary discourse. David McNicoll now joined the select band who were constantly, frequently at awkward times, subjected to Victor's telephonic spate of queries and suggestions. David maintained a courteous and helpful demeanour throughout, and Victor came to like and admire him. As Victor's extant correspondence shows, David tried manfully to satisfy Victor's requirements; Victor's old friends knew from experience that this was no easy task as he was not a man to be easily fobbed off.

Victor's anxieties stemmed from his impression that the SCCC's plans differed from his own understanding of what should be done. In the first place, they asked us to agree that they might spend £50,000 of the grant immediately for administrative purposes, and we had complied, but Victor wanted detailed information about how it was to be spent. Secondly, he was disappointed that the SCCC had not incorporated his own written statements in the Agreement, or at least appended them. Thirdly, as the year 1989 went on, he was unhappy about the lack of progress being made: as the minutes of the trustees' meeting on 31 October 1989 put it, 'the information consultation process, telephone messages and letters, had not produced very much in the way of concrete proposals or action.' His impatience was understandable, but we pointed out that these things took time in official circles: meetings of the Council were held at fairly long intervals, and little could be done without its sanction. As for finance, we could only hope that the consultations promised in the Agreement would allow us to keep an eye on things and help keep matters progressing. But Victor became increasingly agitated about what he saw as dilatoriness and evasiveness. On one occasion, shortly before Christmas, he travelled hastily to Dundee to speak to David McNicoll, who had to be summoned out of a meeting of his Board of Management.

Subsequently Victor wrote to David to apologise, and explained that he was most anxious that the GCF's point of view should be made clear in the SCCC's public utterances. He made a somewhat sinister reference to the grant: 'I thought I had made it clear that if my trustees considered it desirable to suggest any internal re-arrangements in order to simplify the running of our joint venture, my donation would still be devoted to this work on which I have been engaged for a number of years.' In the short, hasty talk they had had, David recalled, Victor was very agitated, and he felt alarmed for his health.

In fact Victor had had another cardiac episode. On 11 January 1990 he wrote again to David: 'I am feeling much better now but am still under a cardiologist and just accepting things as they are.' He soon learned, however, that the SCCC was taking action: the two officers they had assigned to the task, Sydney Smyth and Keith Robinson, had been busy consulting people, writing memoranda, studying available literature on values education; and they were able personally to study values education in action in Toronto. An Interim Position Paper was being drafted, and Victor received a copy in late February. David McNicoll also promised to make Victor's own Background Note available to recipients of the final version. Victor was fairly satisfied with the draft. The authors used the definition of *value* which now commonly appeared in writing about values education: 'a set of principles which are consistent and which inform and direct our actions and activities.' Values listed as examples were compassion, courtesy, freedom, generosity, honesty, justice, loyalty, responsibility, sensitivity and tolerance; and all these, they suggested, could be subsumed within the concept of respect – respect for self, for others and for the environment. Values education must mean making people aware of values and 'critically reflective' of them. This was, more or less, Victor's own language – recognition of the role of values education and listing a selection of the values that might be taught.

Practical recommendations were consistent with Victor's rationale for his Plan. Schools should identify the values by which they stand. Pupils should be provided with opportunities and situations allowing for experiential learning so that abstract values can be translated into a practical guide for living. In the development of values the school should work with the home and the local community. The concept of citizenship should be a key element in values education. Every education authority should draw up a statement of values for schools: key aspects are proposed to provide the basis for such statements: developing an appreciation of learning; developing respect and caring for self; developing respect and caring for others; developing a sense of belonging; developing a sense of social responsibility and care for the environment. An important paragraph states: 'the agreement between the Gordon Cook Foundation and the SCCC is concerned with the promotion and application of values and citizenship in education . . . and it provides a unique opportunity to build upon the important work of the Foundation in the past twenty years and to strengthen and make more explicit the commitment of the Council to these important aspects of education.'

Victor had every reason to believe that this Statement was a triumph for himself personally, a tribute to his work over many years and an open acknowledgement of the educational principles he had striven so hard to establish.

Chapter Eleven

Tributes

On 30 March 1990 the *Times Educational Supplement Scotland* carried an article I had written with the title, 'Aberdeen's enlightened eccentric'. I wrote this piece to give the educational community a picture of a man I had grown to like and respect over many years. The last two paragraphs summed up my own perception of Victor Cook as a man:

> Many people have viewed Victor Cook's work with suspicion. He was sometimes mistakenly associated with Moral Rearmament. His Plan was scoffed at as a wrong-headed programme for manipulating children's minds. But there was nothing sinister about Victor Cook. He never evinced the slightest wish to advance the interests of any political, religious or ideological pressure group. Of course his outlook was to some extent that of an elderly Scots laird, and his set of values could certainly be branded bourgeois and oldfashioned. Of course he was a bit of an eccentric. But when you knew him you learned that he was an earnest, sincere, generous-minded, deep-thinking man. His single-mindedness dwelt amicably alongside an innate diffidence and modesty. His whole life, and his considerable wealth, were genuinely devoted to furthering the mental, emotional and physical welfare of children.
>
> Much of the opposition he met in educational circles came from people who could not accept his ethical dogma. Recently I attended a meeting of the Scottish branch of the Philosophy of Education Society. We heard a paper from Brenda Almond, a distinguished modern philosopher. Her paper argued that modern students of Ethics now acknowledge the existence of 'simple, teachable values' which are held valid in most societies today, and which ought to be an urgent concern of educators in the next decade. I went home thinking how pleased Victor would be when I told him; but there had been a phone call to say he had died.

Victor died on 9 March 1990. It was, as his old friend and trustee, Jack Marshall, observed, 'a low-key event'. He had taken ill suddenly at home, was rushed to hospital and died there: altogether he required medical attention for only two and a half days. It is ironic, but in keeping with his personality, that a brief obituary in the local press made no mention of the Foundation.

He was buried on 16 March, and his trustees, with his lawyers and the executors of his will, repaired to Countesswells House to prepare for a new phase in the history of the Gordon Cook Foundation which he had set up so many years before. His minister and friend (and trustee), Derek Henderson, thanked the executors on behalf of the trustees for showing them round the house, and paid a warm tribute to Victor, both as a person and as a pioneering educator. The lawyers explained that 'the pecuniary legacies looked as though they would amount to some £24,000 and that thereafter the residue of the estate was to go to the Foundation, including Countesswells House and Abergairn'. (Abergairn was a farm-house Victor had owned.) Thereafter 'it would be up to the trustees to determine what to do with the estate, the heritable property and the stocks and shares: it was likely that the amount Mr Cook had left to the Foundation would be of the order of £3 million'. After dealing with some business matters we set in motion the new regime we needed to set up: I proposed Sir Maitland Mackie as chair of the board, and we agreed to meet again in a week's time. It was characteristic of Victor Cook that he left a handsome gift (£500) to each of sixteen 'present or former employees' of his company. He also expressed the wish that Abergairn House should be retained by the trustees for at least fifteen years after his death 'to provide holiday accommodation for those promoting the work of the Foundation or for such other purpose as the trustees may consider appropriate'. In the event we came to the conclusion that it would not be in the interests of the Foundation for us to retain the farmhouse for this or any other purpose, and it was sold in due course. Victor also reminded us that the primary purpose of the Foundation was 'to finance the work of the Plan for Schools entitled "On Citizenship and Health Education"'; but:

in the event of the objects of the Plan becoming general policy and practice in State schools or institutions of higher education, or if at any time the said objects cannot for any reason be satisfactorily achieved the whole funds and assets . . . shall be applied to finance Lectures, annually or at longer intervals to be entitled 'The Gordon Cook Citizenship and Health Lectures' on the subject of the teaching and practice of citizenship values and health education in its widest aspects, or on some allied topic, provided that the identity of the Foundation is maintained, and to finance the printing, publication and dissemination of such lectures in a form suitable for classroom use in schools or institutions of higher education, and also for the making of such awards as the Trustees of the said Foundation may consider appropriate in the field of education, to schools and individuals . . .

The will had been drawn up in September 1988. At that time plans were being discussed for the setting up of a national centre for values education under the joint aegis of the government in Scotland and the Foundation. It was therefore reasonable that Victor should assume that there was a possibility that his Plan's approaches might become 'general policy and practice'. But in 1990 we were not justified in entertaining any such possibility.

Our business now as trustees was to carry on the work of the Foundation, manage the considerable assets we now possessed, and maintain the integrity of the capital against the ravages of inflation, which Victor feared above all else in the financial sphere. Our major duty was to try to reach our own understanding of the Foundation's true purposes, as stipulated by Victor and 'translated', as Jack Marshall put it, into terms that were relevant and effective in the modern educational world. One or two of the trustees, willing as they were to honour our old friend's work, had no real understanding of the nature of moral education: they had read virtually nothing on the subject – not even Victor's own writings – and the language of the submissions that started to come in was beyond them. In their hearts, it seems, they believed that Victor had largely been wasting his money. There was even a proposal that our funds should be vested in a local museum that would portray the life of the city in his youth, and include some kind of information centre. Fortunately, the educationists on the board vetoed that suggestion, pointing out that Victor, in all his writings and discussions, had never envisaged anything remotely like a museum. Victor's life's work was, in a real sense, the antithesis of a museum's purpose: his thought and activity were centred on the future, not the past. To people unfamiliar with his work, particularly lay persons with no knowledge of modern educational ideas and issues, the Foundation under Victor's direction might well have seemed to lack relevance; idealists are often mocked by hard-nosed pragmatists. We have Sir Maitland Mackie's perspective in his entertaining autobiography, *A Lucky Chap* (published by Ardo in 1992):

I have also been involved in a number of charitable trusts. The first was as chairman of the Victor Cook foundation. He was chairman of the firm of Barry, Henry and Cook who made castings in Aberdeen. They made most of the brander covers in the city for example. It was a very good business but in 1970, with the coming of the oil, Mr Cook sold out to Seaforth Maritime for a very good price. He invested the money and all his investments did well ... even better than the company would have done. He was then able to pay full attention to his one great interest in life which was to see that children were educated in the proper way to live. How he thought he knew all about that was hard to understand for he was a bachelor with no children (that we knew of) and a mother complex but nevertheless had a fixed idea that he could tell teachers how to educate children about living properly. He had already given about £200,000 to the Victor Cook Foundation and I was a very early member and tried to help Victor all I could. But he was a very determined man and difficult to advise because he thought he knew exactly what was needed. He had some very good trustees like Jack Marshall, the ex-Gordon's College headmaster, and Dr Bill Gatherer an ex-director of education in the Lothians and latterly Peter Clarke the former head of the Robert Gordon's Institute of Technology and Charles Skene one of Aberdeen's great entrepreneurs. Then there was the Rev Derek Henderson. He had been his minister and came down from Inverness for the regular meetings.

Victor used part-time teachers to help him produce log books to give out to children and leaflets and he gave prizes for the best essays and all sorts of things. All this was planned at Countesswells House where he lived on the outskirts of Aberdeen. Most of his ideas were quite good except that they were out of date. They related to his experiences at school and we found it very difficult to get him to accept the fact that he ought to employ somebody active in modern education to help him make up his leaflets and log books relevant to up to date problems. That used to make him quite angry. Nevertheless we all liked Victor and we wanted to help.

We eventually succeeded in persuading him to get into the colleges of education and get those who were going to be teaching the young to put over his material. We recommended that he should work through the Scottish Education Department and persuade them that this was a necessary part of education. So he gave the Scottish Education Department a quarter of a million pounds to finance a committee who would see if Cook's views constituted a teachable subject or not....

At this time when we thought we were making a little progress the dear old man had a heart attack and died and I was left as chairman of the executors and chairman of his trust fund. He had left the whole of his estate, Countesswells House and grounds and all his investments totalling three and a half million pounds to the fund which had already grown so that the fund is now worth four million pounds. So I now had an embarrassment of riches with which to pursue a somewhat uncertain objective.

All this represented a lay person's perception of Victor and his work; but Mackie's account (no doubt dictated and printed without much care for style) is characteristic of the man: shrewd, egotistical, simplistic, a little condescending, with much more respect for Victor's money than for his ideas, not too scrupulous about accuracy, but fundamentally goodnatured and always genial, with the parochialism and humour of his north-eastern background. He was a good chairman, always ready to listen to his fellow trustees and trying to understand what the experts were saying, anxious to do what was best. But he was deluding himself if he thought that he alone had control of 'an embarrassment of riches', and he was quite wrong to presume that we needed to pursue 'a somewhat uncertain objective'.

In fact we lost no time in furthering some of the main objectives that Victor had entrusted to us. We wrote to a number of teacher training institutions inviting them to submit proposals for research and development projects relating to values education. The letters were drafted by me and approved by the board, and I followed them up with meetings with the principals and their senior staff. We proposed several areas of work: to St Andrew's College we suggested they should continue investigating the feasibility of 'teaching values' to primary school children, work they had begun during Victor's last years. We asked Moray House College (now the education faculty of Edinburgh University) to devise approaches to values education for secondary pupils; in the event this project bifurcated to embrace separate studies of the processes of understanding values and learning how to apply them in other aspects of the curriculum, both focussing on the role of teachers. We commissioned Northern College in Aberdeen to examine and evaluate all of Victor's writings and other materials. (The results of this project form part of Chapter 7.) At an early meeting of the board we agreed to assign substantial grants to each of these projects, covering some three years' work. The choice of Scottish institutions, two of which were under the direction of trustees of the Foundation, was deliberate: this allowed us to supervise the projects in person, and to ensure that action in R and D was swift; it also allowed us to learn directly from the college staff involved what we needed to know about the problems and complexities of developing innovative learning and teaching activities. Inevitably, however, we were thought to be narrowly parochial in our operations for the first few years after Victor's death. This was true, not only because it was easier for us to work with bodies and individuals we knew but also because there were only two of the trustees not based in Aberdeen, and there was a constant tendency for some of the trustees to view the Foundation as an Aberdeen concern, or at best a Scottish concern. This was far from Victor's intentions: he had from the beginning of his campaign thought in the context of the whole of Britain, despite his concentration on Scottish schools during his last years. It was, to some extent, as a counterweight to this parochial tendency that we took an early decision to pursue the idea of a series of lectures in Victor's memory on the subject of values and education.

For this purpose we commissioned a young moral philosopher at St Andrews University, John Haldane, Director of the Centre for Philosophy and Public Affairs. Under Haldane's efficient direction a series of lectures was mounted between 1992 and 1999. Each lecture was delivered at two venues, one in Scotland and one in England. The lecturers, all distinguished philosophers, were invited to address themes related to values and education: they were Lord Quinton and Anthony O'Hear (1992), Baroness Warnock and Richard Pring (1994), Rabbi Jonathan Sacks and Sir Stewart Sutherland (1996), and Mary Midgely and Bryan Appleyard (1999). Thus throughout the 1990s the work of Victor Cook was commemorated in the form of serious discussion of values issues by leading modern thinkers. The purport and potential impact of these lectures can be amply conveyed by the prefatory observations of the editor, John Haldane. Of Quinton and O'Hear he wrote that they

> explored various aspects of the idea of a culture as constituted by intellectual and artistic traditions, traditions partly defined by concerns for excellence of conception and expression. While Quinton sought to defend both the idea of a canon of great works, and the value of making these subjects of study in schools, O'Hear argued that the very notion of objective values as such, is presupposed in our deliberations about how to act as individuals and about what policies – including educational policies – to pursue as a society.

In his introduction to the published lectures of Lady Warnock and Richard Pring he refers approvingly to their qualification, both as philosophers interested in educational theory and as practitioners in higher education, to be able to comment critically on governmental policies and their influence on education:

> thus, as well as learning a good deal about the history of educational policy readers will find themselves drawn into various philosophical reflections about the nature of education and the adequacy of the liberal/vocational contrast, and about the ideas of an educational need and of good teaching.

Introducing the lectures by Jonathan Sacks and Stewart Sutherland, on 'Education, Values and Religion', Haldane's references point to their meditations on the dependence of education on common religious or moral commitments. Sacks discusses the contrasting views of man as a 'political animal' and as a 'social animal': 'the problem for us today is that community seems ever more necessary, yet without some common religious or moral commitments ever more difficult to achieve.' As Sacks pointed out, 'it is increasingly difficult for many people to feel confidence in the very idea of moral and religious values.' Sir Stewart Sutherland, Haldane points out, picks up this general theme, arguing that educational practice rests upon educational philosophy:

> while Sacks begins in the past and looks from there forward, Sutherland starts with a description of the present century as one of 'upheaval, disruption and uncertainty', and suggests that the sources of this can be identified as cultural pluralism, the fragmentation of knowledge and 'moral atomisation'.

Haldane remarks that he offers 'a reworking of the idea that the aim of education is the development of the soul'. It will be seen that these lectures, remote as they may seem from the more practical concerns that preoccupied Victor Cook, nevertheless discuss, with an authority that neither Victor nor any of his trustees could ever aspire to, a number of the central issues thrown up by his proposals and activities.

(The last series of lectures, by Mary Midgely and Bryan Appleyard, dealing with ideas about the assumptions and implications of 'scientistic' styles of thought, were not closely relevant to the preoccupations of the Foundation; but they are valuable contributions to our general understanding of how science relates to human values, and it is easy to see how well they might serve as supporting materials in any collection of the kind of philosophical and discursively practical educational works which Victor hoped to provide to educators.)

John Haldane himself eloquently located Victor's work in a modern philosophical context, not only in his introductions but also in a work written by himself and David Carr, another distinguished young philosopher working in Scotland: this was *Values and Values Education* (1993), published in the same format by the Centre for Philosophy and Public Affairs of the University of St Andrews. (The substance of these important essays is discussed in Chapter 12.)

In his introduction to the 1992 lectures Haldane points to the serious claims that can be made for Victor Cook's life's work:

> Victor Cook's personal contribution to the cause of better education in the field with which he was most concerned took two main forms: first, producing classroom materials for young children in which values, particularly moral ones, might be developed; and second, lobbying politicians, administrators and educationalists in order to have programmes of this sort adopted within schools in Scotland and beyond. . . . Cook's idea of linking values and education was not that of uncommitted analysis . . . He clearly did think that some ways of going on are better than alternatives, and furthermore he believed that those whom society charges with the education of its children have a duty (not a mere permission) to introduce pupils into these ways of going on. In other words, he favoured teaching *in* and *of* values rather than a non-committal study *about* them.

In his introduction to the second lecture series, Haldane paid another significant tribute to Victor's work:

> The person whose life and interest in education this series of lectures commemorates, and through whose benefaction they have been made possible, viz Victor Cook (1897–1990), was strongly committed to the idea that schooling must have as one of its principal aims the inculcation of a sense of values. Unless children acquire an understanding of the difference between right and wrong conduct, good and bad aims and motivations – and a practical sense of which are which – they will not achieve virtue in their personal lives or in their adult role as citizens. There are, then, individual and societal reasons for being concerned about the place of values in education.

Victor's death was marked by a wide variety of tributes, both for commemorating his benefactions and also remembering a remarkable human being. Here is an impression by Neville Stewart, an English authority on further education and a founder of an influential association dedicated to values education:

Victor Cook: a man with a single-minded enthusiasm for values

In May 1989 an article appeared in the *Times Educational Supplement*. It was about values and the formation of NAVET, the National Association for Values in Education and Training. Very soon after the phone went in my office. On the other end was a distinctive Scots voice who introduced himself as Victor Cook. He had read the article and was ringing to declare an interest in the same area. He invited me up to Aberdeen to stay with him and to discuss our common interest. I was to find that to speak of an interest was an understatement. Victor Cook had a great and consuming passion for values, a virtually single-minded enthusiasm which pushed everything else to the circumference.

I arrived in Aberdeen to be met at the station by a person who was relatively frail physically but whose mind and will were anything but frail. I wondered how we would travel given that he was around 90 years of age. I was soon to find out as he led me towards the car park and into his car. He was still driving! Getting the car out of a very crowded station was the first of a sequence of 'interesting' experiences as a passenger in the car. I felt for the second gear as it got so much extra work – we stayed in it for a long time – though the fourth gear must have been relieved! Not only were the driving habits a little eccentric and the reaction speeds reduced but every journey was the opportunity for further exploration of the beloved theme of values. Keen as I am to discuss values, I confess I found it hard to concentrate on a number of occasions!

The welcome was warm at the start and continued to be so. I found myself entering the driveway of what had once been a very grand estate and house. It was obvious it had not had much recent care and attention and the main reason was soon plain. It was now a base for exploring the values scene and provided the basic necessities for Victor who seemed to live a very frugal existence. He had gone to much trouble to make me comfortable and welcome though these were second order matters. What mattered was to make the maximum use of the occasion to explore further his beloved values. He told me the

97

fascinating story of how he came to be interested in the subject and introduced me to his favourite gurus and texts. I came away loaded with a variety of materials. It was clear that he greatly valued the support he had been given from several leading figures in Scottish Education especially Bill Gatherer. He set great store as to what they were going to be able to accomplish together. I can remember two thoughts came into my mind. One was that his great age meant nothing to him. He was planning and striving as if he was in his thirties. The other was that having looked at the curriculum material it was clearly somewhat dated. I did not feel it appropriate in the circumstances to share this thought but wondered how the cause he was so enthusiastic about was going to prosper if it was wedded too closely to such material. I was not then to know the way things would change and open up in the near future. It is a thought I have pondered on that in a very real way the cause so dear to his heart has been able to prosper since his death in a way that was not possible while he was alive. He played a very remarkable John the Baptist role. I was struck by the absence of any ego trip in what he was about. He showed me various items of publicity in which he figured large but it was the forwarding of the values cause that he was excited about, not the personal publicity.

He loved the country around his home and took me to see various places such as Balmoral. But even his love for the places and scenes took second place to his enthusiasm for values. He would interrupt some explanation of historical fact by suddenly sharing the latest idea that had come into his fertile mind about values.

It did not take long to realise that Victor Cook had read and thought much about values. But his enthusiasm was not abstract. He clearly had a love for children and it seemed his real purpose was to enable them to have the opportunity whereby they could be guided to know and to follow what was good and true.

Victor travelled with me for the first part of the journey home. He was off to a meeting with some of those people he had mentioned and who so encouraged him. His enthusiasm was as great as ever and we continued to talk about values issues as we went South. We parted on the train and I spent much of the rest of the journey thinking what a remarkable man I had just had the privilege to share a few days with, a man with a single-minded enthusiasm for values.

A contrasting but no less valuable picture of Victor emerges from an obituary written by Bill Horton, Religious Education Adviser to the Arch-diocese of Glasgow:

> Victor Cook was an optimist, a man of faith, of integrity and tenacity – otherwise he would never have continued to strive in promoting his vision of values education. It would have been so much easier for him to compromise and provide the funding for others to promote current theories of values education. But Victor was made of stern stuff and resolutely over the past twenty years he 'stayed at the helm' in promoting the twelve principles of good citizenship. That's where his faith came in, for he must have felt discouraged at times when his principles were rejected. He refused to have his vision hijacked and he showed his strength of character in the way he continued to lead the Foundation's work right up to his death.
>
> He was a highly intelligent man who could hold his own with academics, but what struck me most about him was his child-like quality – and this was his greatest challenge to others. He wanted to educate young people in the principles of good citizenship so that they would enjoy a happy and fulfilled adult life together. He also wanted to express these principles in a style and language that would be readily accessible to the children – those whom he was seeking to serve. That's where he experienced most of his opposition for most could not accept the child-like way Victor wanted to express his principles.
>
> Yet this child-like quality of Victor is at this time a great source of consolation. In St Mark's Gospel, chapter 10 v 15 states: 'I tell you the truth, anyone who will not receive the Kingdom of God like a little child will never enter it.' We can rejoice therefore that Victor of all people has now entered the Kingdom of God, and we can be sure that he has not stopped working for his vision. Indeed now that he is so close to God, we can be confident that his influence will be even greater in encouraging others to have the desire to give young people a good start in life and to lead them into a happy and fulfilled adult life together. I am grateful to have known Victor even for a short while over these past few years and I will continue to ask him to seek God's help when it seems that the children we are seeking to serve seem to have been forgotten.

By the end of the 1980s the number of persons who had read Victor's own writings was very small; an even smaller number had read his work with the serious intent to reach an understanding of his vision. One of these was Jeff Bagnall, Lecturer in Religious Education at St Andrew's College. Some extracts from his paper, *A Sketch of Victor Cook's Educational Vision*, provide a careful and respectful analysis of Victor's thinking:

> The educational vision of Victor Cook must be discerned from his collection of jottings, quotations and plans. We must also draw on what is remembered of Mr Cook and what is known of his times. And in sketching and highlighting his message we must look to the past, to the context of its origin. Perhaps it is the case with Victor in comparison with other educational pioneers that unwelcome old truths seem pallid without exuberance of language or modernity of terminology. And yet Victor's gentle and respectful approach and his humility among both pupils and educationalists matches well his message of the centrality of personal and interpersonal valuing in the process of formal education.

Times of Tension

A person cannot be caricatured from the times in which he lives but he is cultivated within them and bears some characteristics of his era. Victor was brought up in a time of respect for parents, to be polite in society and to restrain his own inclinations in the face of others in a gentlemanly manner. In the decades prior to the collection of Victor's ideas, education was confident. Indeed it was didactic and dogmatic, despite challenges and experiments to the contrary. Even if the intelligentsia thought otherwise, there was a belief that there were sure truths. Although the seeds of atheistic humanism were scattered, religious practice was still common. While the British Empire discretely dissolved yet imperialism was not a defunct attitude. After the experiences of war and unemployment there was hope in the successes of social reforms and of industrial inventiveness and growth. To top it all permissiveness had entered the ring with unrighteousness. It was a time of tensions between a classic and dynamic view of the world.

Industry and Religion

Victor was surely influenced in his adult life by his industrial experience and his religious interests. From the industrial processes he received confirmation of his belief in the existence of immutable truths and in the importance of conforming to the rules. The mechanisms of industry presupposed reliable and unchanging laws of physics and engineering: good business abides by a contract and completes in time. In industrial relations the example of Robert Owen would not be forgotten. Victor had living proof of the benefit of respecting and caring for others. The process from planning and blueprint, through various methods and techniques combined with vigilance and human labour leading to the marketing of the final product provided a paradigm for the educational process and a foundation for Victor's insistence that with the right methods values can be taught.

Religion brought two buttresses to Victor's vision. Christianity proclaimed eternal truths and absolute moral demands with utter confidence. Yet if this gave him surety about the absoluteness of truths it came with no prophetic extravagance of words. He suffered from neither of Hume's criticisms of religion – from superstitious credulity or fanatical enthusiasm. In addition, Christianity had faith in possibilities; it sought the reform of the sinner. Some Christians angrily condemned and opposed moral depravity, others sought the reform of the sinner by regular forgiveness: underlying both approaches was the belief in the possibility of conversion by the grace of God. Christianity taught that adherence to the moral norms can be instilled, for it is the will of God they should be. While Victor felt assurance of success for his enterprise if only the right methods could be found, he probably believed more in human effort than in grace, more in pelagianism than in predestination.

An Educational Vision

Victor's vision extended into both the theoretical and the practical aspects of modern education. He believed in values common to humanity apart from any religious affiliation. This belief raises the philosophical issue of the existence and nature of such eternal values: and there is also the theoretical question for educationalists as to whether the communication of universal values is an appropriate part of the curriculum, formal or informal. On the more practical side there are other issues: how values come to be embraced by an individual and what role formal education can play in this process. As well as a taxonomy of values there may be needed a developmental structure for values clarification (as it might be called nowadays). The relevant teaching and learning processes would rest upon the resolution of such issues and questions.

Common Human Values

His vision assumed recognition of common human values. Since there may be some philosophical unease with this it must be added that it does not count against his vision. All wide-ranging systems of thought are based upon assumptions: it is for others at later times to suspect and test them. Victor was anxious for this examination of his ideas to take place. It is only recently that critical theory has enabled scholars elaborating generalisations to proceed with great caution in respect of their claims: those with a vision generally don't so proceed and no such attitude is manifest, for example, in the works of Sir Arthur Bryant and William McDougall which Victor was so keen to quote though not accept wholeheartedly...

It is in specifying values, perhaps most of all, that the language of Victor Cook often dulls any empathy with what he is chiefly aiming to say. His naming of 'maturity of character', 'self-discipline', and 'dedication to work' might not be disputed but the terminology has a flavour that is far from visionary. Amongst such language 'delight in beauty', 'kindness and friendship' and 'reasonable citizenship' seem effete and lacking in educational clarity. Whoever tries to abstract from the mode of expression might be disappointed by the absence of any clearcut and orderly list of acceptable values. Yet is not this the sign of the frontier that Victor envisaged? – a lack of dogmatism and utter respect for the values of others?...

A Paradoxical Vision

Victor is struggling to find a method that will be true to the tension of his – the vision that the child's individuality must be respected and that there are common values that need to be taken on board. It is because of this tension that he needs faith that a methodology can be found. It is in this context that the methods he suggested must be viewed. They are tentative proposals intended to be illustrative of his key thrust: they are to be tested against practice. This was what Victor wanted for them and why he recorded favourable examples of the use of his ideas. This search for a way of putting his insight into practice shows itself in some of the projects of the Gordon Cook Foundation that he was able to set up before he died. It was also because he recognised the difficulty of expressing his central vision that he wanted control over the Foundation's work to be in the hands of people who knew him well. They are concerned with the philosophical, educational, resource and implementation aspects of Victor Cook's insight. A vision of a tension elusive equally to rhetoric and technical language, a vision embodied in a life marrying firmness and gentleness, resolve and hesitancy. Victor's was a vision of paradox now on the threshold of reality – a paradox of reasoned confidence and unpretentious practice.

These excerpts from educationalists interested in the teaching of moral values and familiar with the philosophy of moral education make it clear that Victor Cook's writings carry a burden of serious reflection on the subject. It is also apparent that his influence as an instigator of action in research and development was being acknowledged in a manner that would have been greatly pleasing to him in his lifetime. At the same time, he went to his death still dissatisfied with the progress made in his campaign. When I was interviewed by the Dundee newspaper *The Courier* shortly after his death I tried to be frank about the obstacles that lay in his path during his long struggle to establish moral teaching in schools. The subsequent article, it seems to me, offers a fair and vivid picture of the man (though with hindsight I am sure they overstated some of my remarks!). It is, however, reproduced here as a whole mainly because it showed how far the Foundation still had to go in our efforts to fulfil his bold ideas in a practicable form.

Victor Cook, the Aberdeen millionaire industrialist who died in March this year, has left the bulk of his £3 million estate to the Gordon Cook Foundation, which he set up, in his mother's name, in 1974 to improve the character development of children. Here, one of the foundation's trustees, Dr William Gatherer, retired chief adviser in education to Lothian Regional Council, tells 'The Courier' about Victor Cook and his lifelong dream – to help children grow up good citizens.

If Victor Cook had achieved his first ambition to be a teacher, his impact on the education system would probably have been negligible, confined to one class at one school at any given time.

Instead, he was made to go into his father's engineering firm, and the frustration he was to feel at viewing his chosen profession from the outside, and as an amateur, provided the inspiration for the Gordon Cook Foundation.

There were obstacles, however, on the road to realising his ambition, for while Victor Cook was universally regarded as a kindly, conservative, bachelor philanthropist, his ideas were sometimes misinterpreted by people suspicious of his crusading zeal.

Dr Gatherer was less than equivocal about his first impression of the well-intentioned amateur – an impression he did not spare Mr Cook. 'I told him I thought he was a bit of a crank and an amateur who should not be interfering with work that should be done by professional teachers.

'He was very interested in education and politics, and he was quite convinced that we need to teach young people to be good citizens. He was a generous-hearted man, keen to help young people to grow up better able to cope with life and to contribute to the needs of society. In a sense, he was a frustrated teacher.

'He wrote to many people about his views, including Edward Heath when he was Prime Minister, and he got a lot of support from various people, but the person who gave him most encouragement was Lord Reith of the BBC, who shared his views. Victor took it very well when I told him I thought he was a crank. He was very willing to listen to advice from professionals in education and he read everything he could on moral education and citizenship.

'I realised then that, although he was a bit of a crank, he was also very sincere. I agreed with his general educational objectives, as most educationalists would – and his desire for a return to old-fashioned values often missing from family life is becoming increasingly popular nationally.'

Victor took some advice, then went to a lawyer and put down £100,000, decreeing that the income from the money would pay for the production of materials for schools.

'That's what we are doing now, commissioning projects from professional researchers and developers on a wide range of topics to give youngsters the opportunity to discuss ideas and moral dilemmas and world studies – an awareness of Third World problems and what we can do to help – and to offer health education.

'Victor prepared some material himself, but it was very amateurish. We used to argue about that a lot. The work has to be professional. Children are much more sophisticated these days and need things to be well presented.'

Since its inauguration, the foundation has been working steadily towards the goal of seeing every school in the country receiving, and using, its materials. 'Some material has already gone out to schools, mainly in the Aberdeen area, but it didn't exactly catch on like wildfire, largely because it wasn't good enough. As an area of study in the curriculum, it is only beginning to become recognised.

'Two years ago, Victor approached the then minister for education at the Scottish Office, Mr Forsyth, and made a £200,000 contribution to the Scottish Consultative Committee on the Curriculum, who are producing a document which will be sent out to every school in the country.

'We want to follow up that document with really first-class material prepared by professionals and propose to spend about £150,000 a year on professional materials from colleges of education.'

The foundation has also funded a research and development project at St Andrew's College of Education, Glasgow. 'They have got quite a number of schools interested.'

The most remarkable thing about the foundation, though, is the fact that it is the result of one man advocating his own ideas, and doing so with such conviction that he has won the support of many influential people. The list of foundation trustees includes Sir Maitland Mackie; John Marshall, retired headmaster of Robert Gordon's College; the Rev. Roderick Henderson; Former Robert Gordon's Institute for Technology Principal Dr Peter Clarke; David Adams, principal of the Northern College; B. J. McGettrick, principal of St Andrew's College, Glasgow; and Charles Skene, chairman of the Aberdeen-based Skene Group.

Nonetheless, Dr Gatherer anticipates a certain degree of suspicion on the part of schools when they first receive the foundation's material. 'But if the materials are good in the eyes of the teachers, then they will use them. I have great faith in teachers – they are the best people to decide the value of our materials to their own pupils. We are not concentrating on any particular age group, but at the entire range of schooling, and further education as well.'

Victor Cook really felt for youngsters whom he believed were not getting the best type of up-bringing at home.

'He didn't dwell on negative subjects like violence and vandalism, but felt they were perpetrated by youngsters who had not been educated as well as they should have been and had not been given the support they should have got. He was always very optimistic and cheerful.

'His view of the future was a romantic one, with every youngster getting an education that allowed him to fulfil his own potential in life, and to have a great deal of human sympathy for the plight of others.'

Despite the obviously high ideals Victor Cook sought to promote, he was not without his detractors.

'Some people thought, mistakenly that Victor was in touch with Moral Rearmament. That made some people hostile until they realised how sincere and genuine and independent he was.

'He was also criticised because a lot of his ideals were a bit old-fashioned. Some teachers were suspicious and sceptical about teaching values in schools. What happens when they conflict with what the youngster gets at home? That's why Victor believed schools have to work in partnership with parents.

'All the teachers who met him were very impressed by him, and children in the schools loved him.

'There's also the fact that values education under different names is a great favourite with dictatorships all over the world, in Communist and Fascist countries, for example. That was not Victor's idea at all.

'Neither are his ideas strictly political. He was a staunch Conservative but his ideas had the support of members of all parties. In fact, he was in correspondence with Len Murray when he was general secretary of the TUC.'

Victor Cook has long been regarded as one of the few contemporary philanthropists. By willing the bulk of his estate to the foundation, he is not only furthering the ideals he believed will make for a better future. He is also fulfilling a dream.

Chapter Twelve

Towards a theory of values education

True to his undertaking to Victor Cook, David McNicoll, chief executive of the SCCC, swiftly began the process of fulfilling the agreement between the Council and the GCF. In their press release about the Agreement the Council, represented by David McNicoll and Keith Robinson, a former Director who was being employed on a part-time basis to oversee the values education programme, frankly stated that Mr Cook, as a further commitment to his work on values education, had recently donated £200,000 to the SCCC, the main purpose being to assist the Council to promote and apply principles of Values and Citizenship in Education within Scotland. They described 'Values in Education' (a term that neither Victor nor any of his trustees habitually used) as 'commonly admired human values, attitudes and modes of behaviour which embrace and transcend individual convictions, cultures, nations, faiths and religions world-wide'. This description had certainly won a cautious endorsement from Victor himself, and his trustees had readily accepted it. Their definition of citizenship as 'the attributes, knowledge and social skills which enable young persons to develop into active and useful members of the community in which they live' was equally acceptable. They stated unequivocally that these concepts were already 'consistent with stated positions in a number of SCCC publications and with the objectives of several courses promulgated by the national examinations board'. What was new, it emerged, was that the SCCC now intended to 'promote and apply the principles of Values and Citizenship within ongoing curriculum development programmes'. Review and Development Groups had been set up to implement the government's Curriculum and Assessment 5–14 Programme, and these would examine 'contexts relevant to values in education'. They promised to establish 'one or more centres' where 'published and unpublished materials, including those developed by the Gordon Cook Foundation' would be held and maintained, and to ensure that teachers, and teachers' centres, would have easy access to the assembled materials.

In February 1991 the SCCC published *Values in Education: an SCCC Paper for Discussion and Development*, and issued it to all Scottish schools, school boards, directors of education, colleges of education, universities, professional associations and the press. This was a comprehensive publication of the subject that had occupied the minds of Victor Cook and his trustees for a quarter of a century. There was no mention of the Gordon Cook Foundation, only a hint that it was Cook's money that had brought about the enterprise. This was by no means contrary to the wishes of the Trustees: we never sought explicit acknowledgement of our funding; we were fully aware, moreover, that it was advantageous to our purposes that the publication should be seen as 'official' and part of the government's general efforts to enhance educational development. At the same time, some of the trustees felt that there was something ungracious to Victor's memory in this bland appropriation of his life's work. (The plan to initiate a series of memorial lectures, however, went a long way to mitigate this disappointment.)

The document proposed a number of 'Issues for Discussion'. Under the heading 'The Nature of Values', the working definition which had been given in the Agreement was suggested: *Values are principles or sets of principles which are consistent and which inform and direct our actions and activities.* An important observation follows:

> Values are integral to education: in our teaching we select certain elements of our culture and ignore others, so in according esteem to those elements we reflect the values of our educational system. Everything we do in schools reflects and communicates values. And because we nowadays want to question curriculum policies, which carry powerful implications for the values which the education system serves and seeks to promote, it is important to determine, as far as we are able, what values we adopt, communicate and promote, and then to decide consciously and explicitly what values we *should* adopt, *should communicate* and *should* promote.

This was a clear, direct and powerful call for what we now call values-driven policies and curricula. Acknowledging that some people, to avoid controversy, think it is better to leave values unexamined, and that to examine values, for example in the school curriculum, can create apprehension, and that 'even to attempt to describe and define values in education, or in social and personal life, is to enter a controversial area', the document courageously presents what amounts to a manifesto for values in education:

The Council believes that at national, regional and school levels there should be consideration of values so that they may become a principal criterion for the conduct of our educational affairs: which values are promoted, how they are conveyed and the contexts in which they are acquired; relationships among learners, between teachers and learners, among teachers and between the school and the community. Similar considerations should, of course, shape policy-making; and policy-makers at whatever level should be accountable to society in terms of values.

If this declaration had been taken up seriously, and its implications properly explored, openly and systematically, at all levels in the education system, Scotland would have become a world leader in educational progress. But it never was: neither at that time nor subsequently were values in policy or in school curriculum delivery given the attention the authors of this paper were recommending. More than ten years later, the study of values implicit in the system and the processes of explicating desired values and methods of applying them are being taken up in many education systems throughout the world, but in Scotland – despite the strenuous efforts of the Gordon Cook Foundation and many of its allies and adherents – there is still very little awareness among the politicians or their servants. While it is true that many schools now try hard to put values and citizenship at the heart of their endeavours, they are given little support from the authorities at national or local levels.

The SCCC paper goes on to suggest that, although there is no likely agreement about the ultimate authority for the values we adopt in education, every school should aim to produce 'a clear and dynamic statement of values essential to the wellbeing of all its pupils and the society in which they are growing up'. With this in mind, the SCCC had discussed and formulated a 'statement of position as an expression of its own sense of the values it seeks to promote'. This is put forward as a 'starting point' for similar statements which it was hoped would be produced by education authorities and schools. The authors of the paper expect that 'through processes of discussion, amendment and adjustment to the needs of individual communities, clearer understandings of and commitment to shared values will emerge'.

The so-called Statement of Position on Values in Education comprises a brief list of values which the Council commits itself to promoting in Scottish education. Regrettably, the list is just a list, unsupported by elaborations or exemplifications, and the items are generalised and trite.

For example, 'Appreciation of Learning' is described as 'a commitment to learning', 'a developing understanding of the nature of knowledge', 'self-discipline' and so on; and similar sub-lists are offered for 'Respect and Caring for Self', 'Respect and Caring for Others', 'A Sense of Belonging'; and 'Social Responsibility'. This kind of clichéd catalogue – commonplace in American high schools (and in fact some of the text was imported from Canada) – could hardly command much respect from teachers looking for practical guidance and explanations which would help them in their teaching.

One of our leading educational philosophers, David Carr, lost no time in launching a critical attack on the SCCC's paper, expressing disappointment that it failed to provide 'a clear conceptual framework in terms of which any coherent discussion of these difficult matters might be conducted.' (This was in an article in the *Times Educational Supplement* of 5 April 1991.) Carr pointed out that the given 'working definition' of values was inadequate: many of our values are not consistent, and many guiding principles cannot be called values. He wrote that 'values are dispositions to *choose* conduct, not merely to be directed', and he scoffed at the paper's bland assumption that all that is needed is for people to put together a list of values which can be agreed upon. He showed that the SCCC seemed to vacillate between 'at least three different accounts of the provenance of values: values as personal tastes, predilections or preferences; values as a function of social convention, consensus or agreement; and values derived in some rather more basic way from considerations about fundamental human nature'. He suggested that the paper obviously inclined to the second definition because of the authors' 'constant emphasis (tinged with scepticism) on the importance of agreement, accountability and the need for values to adapt to social change'. Carr himself, as a moral philosopher, asserts 'the proper basis for the educational promotion of such values as honesty, tolerance, compassion and respect for others is that they are morally *right* . . . not that they are upheld by consensus or common humanity'.

The trustees of the GCF welcomed the SCCC paper as an explicit call for the clarification and discussion of the values which we were appointed to promote. Whatever its imperfections as an essay in values education we were glad to see the appearance of questions we wanted teachers to be asking. But it was clear to some of us, as it had been clear to Victor Cook, that the most important questions related to social and moral values. We wanted to encourage the study and application of the values which best inspire students to understand and develop their own conduct as young citizens, to learn the language of moral discourse, and to commit themselves to playing a part in the betterment of the world they were preparing to enter as adults. It was therefore pleasing to see David Carr's article, and we were eager to recruit him and other leading thinkers in the field to help us in our work. Consequently we invited David Carr and John Haldane each to write a brief theoretical work which would answer in authoritative terms some of the questions that were currently exercising teachers and others. In the Preface to the publication that followed (*Values and Values Education*, Centre for Philosophy and Public Affairs, University of St Andrews, 1993) I formulated the questions as follows: 'What exactly do we mean by "values"? If we don't know what values are, how can we teach them? And *WHAT* values, *WHOSE* values, are we to teach? *ARE* there common values? If so, what are they?'

Both of these essays addressed the central questions. They constituted an important philosophical justification for the teaching of moral reasoning and the identification of the moral and social values which express the character of a modern democratic civilisation, and they are still excellent sources of understanding for teachers. John Haldane concentrates on the nature of values. He postulates three levels of thought and expression about values. There are elementary or 'ground-floor' questions, such as 'Is friendship good?' or 'Is honesty always the best policy?' – questions felt by most of us to be easily answered which hardly merit discussion, but which in truth can be philosophically very difficult. For example, virtually everyone would agree that torturing animals for pleasure is not permissible, but if we proceed to ask 'Why is it wrong?' we reach a level of thought which deals with the basis and content of value judgements; and this brings us to a higher, first-floor level of theorising, where we ask what, if anything, makes things good (or bad). At this level, Haldane argues, there are three broad categories of answers. First, the *theological*: something is good if God approves it, and bad if God disapproves of it. Second, there is the *deontological*: certain things, such as actions or states of affairs, are good or bad in and of themselves; these things are classified as types of behaviour – for example, lying is a kind of action that is always morally wrong. Third, there is *consequentialist* value theory: something is good to the extent that it promotes states of affairs held to be good on their own account; an action is right in so far as it results in good consequences. Unlike the deontologist, the consequentialist can only answer the question whether a type of action is right or wrong by looking at instances, at individual actions for example, and then try to construct an answer on that basis. Haldane then poses the questions: are deontological and consequentialist theories descriptions of an independent order of objective goods and requirements, or are they merely accounts of the underlying patterns of our thoughts and attitudes about values? This brings us to the second and highest floor in thinking about values, where we are involved in arguments for and against objectivism and subjectivism. These two philosophical perspectives are central to an understanding of the problems that beset values education. If values are purely subjective, there is no point in teaching about them. But Haldane answers the crucial question 'Are values objective?' with a comprehensive explication of the 'empiricist orthodoxy' which is now the established philosophical perception of the nature of reality. His arguments are presented so cogently and comprehensively that a concise summary here would fail to do them justice. Suffice it to state that he provides a powerful justification for regarding values as having objective validity. The commonplace challenges to this idea, he writes, can all be rationally refuted. It is simply *not* the case that there is widespread disagreement about values, as even a cursory study of modern philosophy will demonstrate. Our beliefs about values are *not* socially conditioned: of course they are formed through social influences and education, but the source of our beliefs is independent of their objectivity. Claims about values certainly express attitudes of approval, but this is only to be expected: 'just as John believes "p" because it is true and not vice versa, so John approves of "x" because it is good and not vice versa.' It is often maintained that claims about values rest on unproven assertions, but this is not obviously so: we can support our claims about the goodness of persons, actions, institutions and so on by showing how these are connected with human flourishing. (And, anyway, all justifications and proofs rest on basic assumptions, and value judgements are no worse off in this respect than other claims.) It is often said that disputes about values cannot be resolved, but that is nonsense: they can often be resolved in real life, as is evident by such marks of civilisation as schools, parks, medicine, democracy. Nor is it true that values are not to be found in nature. That is exactly where they are to be found: they are features or characteristics of actions or states of affairs; they are natural phenomena associated with human nature.

It is difficult to imagine how anyone who has not had some education in moral knowledge and reasoning could sensibly engage in debate about values education. Yet that was the normal condition of many people who wrote and debated about values education in the early 1990s, and it is still largely the case. It was mistakenly believed that some supporters of the GCF were intent upon erecting moral education as a specific subject to be taught by specialists in classrooms. At a conference held under the aegis of the GCF in April 1991 a senior curriculum development officer praised the SCCC discussion paper for not being a paper on moral philosophy, having been written by curriculum developers for an audience unlikely, in the main, to be interested in philosophy. Some years later an SCCC paper called *Values in Education: The Importance of the Preposition* attacked the belief that 'a good dose of values education would do Scottish pupils no harm, if by that we mean a lump of good, old-fashioned, timetabled classroom-based experience on a Tuesday afternoon'. Although most people who wrote on the subject used the terms 'values education' and 'values in education' inter-changeably it was felt that it was important to emphasise that a schools values education programme should not be seen as an add-on specialist discipline to be taught in classrooms like religious education or other academic subjects. Very few people disagreed with that. But the same paper claimed that 'the values dimension' developed critical thinking and judgements, taught pupils to be 'explicit about the values of society', provided young people with a sound foundation on which to base moral and ethical decisions and behaviours, and helped them to be 'capable of thinking', 'exploring', 'reflecting and developing a point of view', without explaining how that could be done without reflective discussion of the kind advocated by Victor Cook and his supporters.

This kind of public scepticism illustrated a change in the posture of the SCCC towards the campaign for moral education that Victor Cook had engaged in during his lifetime. While David McNicoll was chief executive of the SCCC it was openly committed to developing values education in all its aspects as laid down in the Agreement that accompanied the acceptance of a very large donation of money – including, of course, 'consideration' of stated values within the schools and urging schools to 'engage in the discussion of values' with pupils. In an address at a world congress on comparative education in October 1991 in Budapest, McNicoll gave his own personal testimony about education in values:

> I have little faith in the effectiveness of imposing educational or moral values from the top down. Equally I have little faith in the effectiveness of relying on individuals, young or old, to work out their own values and inflicting them on their peers – the bottom-up approach. . . . my personal belief is that values – in education as in life – are most effectively progressed through processes of consultation, discussion and a seeking after consensus . . .

This common-sense view echoed the approaches advocated many years before in the old CCC's reports on social and personal education, and it represents what is undoubtedly the majority view among moral educators today about values education: that it should encompass both learning from informed discussion and activity that builds up 'character', such as all that forms the informal curriculum – games, clubs, meetings – and all that is conveyed by the 'invisible' curriculum – discipline, role models, personal relationships, the learning environment.

But every substantive contribution to the functions of schools needs to be justified in terms of its potential for adding to students' physical, intellectual and moral growth, and to be couched in terms sufficiently persuasive to convince governments and future policy reformers that it is worthwhile. For that reason, among others, it seemed to us essential that values education should be defended by authoritative educational thinkers. Haldane's exposition of the nature of values and his convincing arguments for their objective reality in our lives was – and still is – a valuable support for reflective educators at all levels. David Carr's essay deals with the different philosophical perspectives which have led to important developments in educational theory and practice in respect of the kinds of knowledge and moral powers which our educational enterprises strive to impart. He is concerned with the purposes of schooling as these are identified from generation to generation. In what he calls 'educational traditionalism' the school system aims in large measure to promote certain intrinsically valuable states or dispositions of knowledge and virtue; it regards education as 'a matter of transmission from one human generation to the next of all that is generally thought to be worth preserving in a given culture' – what Matthew Arnold called 'the best that is known and thought in the world'. On this view, values education is concerned with the acquisition of 'intrinsically worthwhile forms of rational knowledge and moral goodness'. In different versions of traditionalism there have been different ways of attesting to the intrinsic authority of ultimate values. They may be founded on religious revelation: things are good if God approves of them or bad if God disapproves. They may derive from charismatic leadership, as in dictatorships. They may be attributed to moral intuition; or they may rest simply in the conviction that what has sustained and given meaning to the lives of our ancestors should be regarded as having actual or potential value for generations to come.

In more recent times opposing philosophies have derived from 'progressivist' and 'radicalist' views. Classical or libertarian progressivism gave rise to the kind of child-centred teaching associated with Rousseau and many more modern educationists such as John Dewey and the members of the committee that produced the seminal Plowden Report and the Scottish Primary Memorandum of the 1960s: according to this approach education is mainly concerned with the knowledge and values which help young people to cope with the challenges of growing up in a changing and often troubled world. Educational radicalism holds that the real value of knowledge and moral education is that it equips individuals with power to control their own affairs. Both these forms of 'anti-traditionalism', Carr points out, are 'instrumentalist' in that they deny that there are certain forms of knowledge, character and conduct which are of 'absolute human value in their own right regardless of their possible pay-off in practical or instrumental terms'. Carr argues for a 'middle way' in the form of 'liberal traditionalism', which combines a healthy reverence for bygone wisdom and past accomplishments with a proper recognition that past achievements are not the last word on any matter but are susceptible of criticism, development and transcendence in the light of fresh insights and new discoveries concerning what is true, right and good in human affairs.

Both Carr and Haldane offer important reassurance to those of us who have worked towards the fulfilment of Victor Cook's aspirations. Haldane's defence of the reality of moral values – arguments which are widely supported by other modern philosophers – merits intensive study by teachers and their advisers; and Carr's critical exposition of the thought which underlies our reasons for educating as we do points us towards a rationale which is nowadays endorsed by practically everyone who thinks seriously about our education systems. We may not be able to justify our convictions in the powerful language of the philosophers, but we know that we want our young people to understand the world they live in and to commit themselves to values which are valid and authentic, and we want to help them attain these values by means of rational enquiry and productive experience; and we want them to express these values in their own personal conduct throughout their lives.

A GCF-sponsored 'workshop' in Harrogate in April 1991 was an important event for the Foundation. It had been organised by our newly appointed chief executive, Bill Robb, and myself, and we had invited representatives from the three curriculum councils in England, Wales and Northern Ireland, as well as some distinguished leaders in the field of moral and values education. The resulting report was significant in several ways. It was edited and published by Bill Robb in an attractive format which the Foundation continued to employ for many years; it represented a new and welcome relationship between the Foundation and some major figures in the educational world; and it added to our collegial network a number of highly influential individuals who shared our perceptions and enthusiasms. Barbara Wintersgill from the National Curriculum Council for England, Una O'Kane from the Northern Ireland Curriculum Council, and Denis Stewart from the Curriculum Council for Wales all contributed valuably to our awareness of the state of affairs outside Scotland; and Denis, in particular, has continued to be an important ally – he is now a director of Learning and Teaching Scotland (LTS). Above all, our deliberations benefited hugely from the contributions of scholars such as Brenda Almond, then Reader in Philosophy and Education at the University of Hull, Helen Haste from the University of Bath, Mal Leicester from the University of Warwick, Monica Taylor from the National Foundation for Educational Research (NFER), and Peter Tomlinson from Leeds University: all in their own way added to the pool of expert experience and knowledge which was gradually spreading throughout the UK.

Brenda Almond's paper, *Seven Moral Myths* (a version of a paper which had appeared in the journal *Philosophy* in 1990), offered an approach to moral education which, she said, 'was concerned with the question of how to live, both as an individual and as a contributor to the shape of society'. She suggested that educators who dealt with this question too often offer 'a smorgasbrod of moral fare' rather than an approach that assumes commitment to some simple fundamental values based on a common human nature. Behind this mistaken practical approach lie certain 'moral myths' or errors of moral reasoning. These included 'relativism', the view that right and wrong, and even truth and falsehood, vary with the opinions of particular persons or groups. This often leads to an excessive degree of toleration generated by the notion that moral judgements may vary according to people's general beliefs about things. If people believe that lying is wrong, for example, they must condemn it; 'toleration requires only that they do not interfere, not that they refrain from judgement.' Another view embedded in the relativist position is that it is necessary to take a value-neutral stance when dealing with, for example, personal relationships with young persons: 'learner-oriented approaches do not have to convey what I would call the "wild autonomy" message that it does not matter what they conclude or what they do – particularly if added to this is the further message: we do not know what they should do.' Another common myth is the assumption that what the majority says/believes is the standard of right and wrong. Liberalism must not be equated with permissiveness: it is a position of principle, a strong moral principle which includes certain strong positive values. 'Too much minding of our own moral business can lead to having none to mind.' She called for a bold new commitment to 'simple teachable values' – a call that might have deeply gratified Victor Cook. We should abjure the temptation to think that what is simple must be intellectually disreputable:

> We would do better, in both values research and moral education, to acknowledge a commitment to humanist tradition that, far from being a bourgeois blemish on the surface of capitalism, is as old as the recorded intellectual history of human beings. This is to acknowledge that, as well as an educational goal, we want the future to be like the past in this respect: that it should contain at least some people who share this commitment, are prepared to live by these values, and who will not be afraid to say that those who disagree with them are wrong.

These strong philosophical reinforcements to the Foundation's central purposes – that we should promote moral education in the various forms indicated to us by our Founder – were to some extent dissipated by our reluctance to embark upon a quixotic campaign to fight against the established norms of educational development in the 1990s. While we remained constant in our desire to devote our funds to projects that might 'make the world a better place', we felt able to support a wide range of disparate enterprises, in the belief that the values we stood for were both manifold and diverse. We were advised by important consultants that we should 'go with the grain' and avoid being dismissed as well-heeled cranks. Our main endeavours for the next several years would have to be pragmatic: encourage values education wherever we found it in whatever form seemed productive; continue to win the respect of the educational leadership; encourage more, and more powerful, thinking about education in values; and continue, among ourselves, to work out what our duties as Victor's trustees enjoined us to do, always now in the light of our own interpretations of his requirements.

Charles Skene OBE DBA

David A. Adams MA

Dr Peter Clarke CBE

William A. Gatherer
MA PhD

Rushworth Kidder

David S. C. Levie
BL NP

Professor Bart
McGettrick OBE KCHS

Sir Maitland Mackie
CBE LLD

John Marshall MA

Introducing the McSmith Family (see p. 50)

An episode from 'The McSmiths'

Gavin T. N. Ross DA MA RIAS FRSA

Victor Cook
(on the right)
and Bill Gatherer
(on the left) with
Professor Urie
Bronfenbrenner,
Loch Lomond,
1978

Chapter Thirteen

The campaign in the nineties

The 1990s was, on the face of things, not a propitious period for innovative education, particularly of the kind that values education represents – putting emphasis on the 'softer' aspects of schooling, the teaching of social and moral values, encouragement of activities like school and class councils, debates, sharing decision making, projects on serving the community and so on. Government policies were firmly centralist and pragmatic: in England the Education Reform Act (ERA) of 1988 was being implemented, and its statutory national curriculum was being driven through by ministers dedicated to the ideology of the New Right, regardless of the protests of teachers and the liberal public. Its consumerist message was being pushed in Scotland by Michael Forsyth, whose policies included the privatisation of educational services, the break-up of the larger education authorities, and a stronger emphasis on teacher appraisal and the sacking of teachers found to be incompetent. Government assumed greater central control to ensure the efficacy of new national tests, the setting of targets for attainment, the skewing of the curriculum towards the conventional, traditional disciplines of language learning, Mathematics and Science – the subjects deemed most useful for the economic improvements the country needed. Yet, paradoxically, the values education movement flourished during the decade; and in this the Gordon Cook Foundation played a not inconsiderable part.

Under Sir Maitland Mackie's chairmanship we proceeded to put the Foundation on a more professional footing than had been achieved when Victor Cook was in charge. The first important step taken was the appointment of a chief executive who would be responsible to the trustees for the implementation of our policies and set up working procedures; he would be assisted by an executive officer and part-time secretarial assistance. Our secretary, Marianne Knight, was made the executive officer. She had been an excellent secretary since just after Victor's death; quietly efficient, hardworking, highly intelligent, with the interests of the Foundation and all the trustees individually very much at heart. But she was not a professional educator, and the majority of the trustees were anxious to place the running of the Foundation in the hands of someone who would combine administrative competence with some knowledge of the educational scene. The person appointed, William M. Robb, seemed to meet these requirements to a satisfactory degree: he had been a member of the Continuing Education department at Glasgow University, and both in South Africa and in Scotland he had gathered some knowledge of business. He quickly assumed command of our small office-suite in Northern College, Aberdeen, and began to familiarise himself with the day-to-day affairs, dealing with correspondence, preparing reports, and reading a wide variety of materials related to the Foundation's sphere of interest. Bill Robb was a hard worker. He studied numerous documents, including curriculum papers, and on this basis produced a 'review of values education in Scotland'. He attempted an analysis of the trust deed Victor had left us and in cooperation with some of the trustees he wrote a 'definition' of values education which was incorporated in publicity material. We allowed him access to a limited amount of funds so that he could commission work without formal reference to the board of trustees, and with this power he obtained a number of essays from prominent people on aspects of the Foundation's remit. He organised the conferences we held in 1991 in Glasgow and Harrogate to discuss our plans with directors of projects and potential associates of the Foundation.

From 1990 to 1996 the Foundation achieved considerable success in winning the attention of the educational world to our purposes. The major advantage we had was our association with the SCCC, which allowed us to develop links with professionals and institutions throughout Scotland, while the support of our colleagues from the Harrogate conference helped us in the rest of the UK. Our dealings with the SCCC staff were not always as productive as some of us would have wished, but they were usually amicable; the continuing presence of Bart McGettrick on both bodies was a great help. As we had hoped when we persuaded Victor to initiate the agreement with the SCCC, the collegial link went far to legitimate our activities, and it gave us a minor part to play in all the major curriculum developments in Scotland. In both the 5–14 Programme and the 'Higher Still' programme values education as represented by the GCF won some measure of recognition. But the SCCC were constrained by government policy to concentrate on developments which had been agreed within the system, and values education *as such* had not been accorded priority. The Council's responsible officers, Ian Barr and Margaret McGhie did, however, substantially advance the general aims of *values in education*, the term which, in their view, was more in tune with the government's perspectives: it seemed to distinguish between *values education* as a separate subject and a general care for commonly approved values in the whole life and work of the school. The bold declarations of the McNicoll era had receded with his retirement. The term *principles* now replaced the term *values* in the documentation, and the whole values approach was embedded in a general advocacy of personal and social education. All this was in part the result of a certain public distaste for explicit consideration of values in schooling. It seems that the *Values in Education* discussion document had not been warmly received by teachers or in the Inspectorate, who were preoccupied by fresh demands upon them for greater 'quality assurance' and more methodical assessment of teachers' performance. But thanks to the SCCC the Review Groups set up to develop guidance on the curriculum in primary and secondary schools (all of whom had received copies of the discussion paper) were encouraged to discuss the role of values in teaching, and the impact of the paper was evinced in all the guidelines (except for Mathematics). Margaret McGhie, who had been appointed to develop thinking and practice in values education, devoted most of her time to the theme in its various guises, for example in Personal and Social Education (PSE), Guidance, Citizenship, and the development of 'school ethos'. In seminars and conferences, Ian and Margaret promulgated the central messages of the campaign for more attention to values as an integral part of the education process, and urged teachers to be aware of their role in communicating values. They should confer to discuss the nature of values, asking themselves what values they communicate and what values they would want to communicate: 'One of the tasks of the SCCC and others engaged in thinking about this area must, of course, be to devise means by which this process may practically be carried out, while avoiding frustrating argument.' They did not rule out the possibility that teachers might accord a special place in their classrooms to discussion of values:

> The position of the classroom teacher must surely be one of the most powerful and autonomous imaginable. Once the classroom door is closed, what happens is his or her sole domain. A classroom teacher, aware of his/her position as a powerful role model and of his/her personal influence on students' values acquisition might wish carefully to structure a values dimension into the learning/teaching process . . .

They explicitly endorsed the notion of 'the teacher as moral agent' and urged schools to pay more attention to the opportunities that are available for equipping themselves to provide more effective programmes for developing the social and personal qualities that make for good citizens.

The Heart of the Matter, published by the SCCC in 1995, is a thoughtful study of the ways in which schools can cater for the personal and social development of their pupils. Education for personal and social development, it states, 'is essentially concerned with the development of a set of inter-related qualities and dispositions and the skills and understandings which are essential if they are to be realised'. It reiterates the values which the earlier SCCC papers had listed as being central to the enterprise – but significantly it calls these 'qualities or dispositions' which 'will be generally acknowledged as fundamental to any recognisable form of moral life' and to 'the prospering of a just and democratic society'. It elaborates the 'qualities' – 'respect, care for others, social responsibility, commitment to learning, and a sense of belonging' – but so far as the question of how these are to be taught is considered the paper confines itself to generalised objectives: a 'positive whole-school climate and ethos', the 'appropriate consideration of aspects of personal and social development in and across curricular areas and subjects', the need for 'progression and coherence in the curriculum'. Other publications are equally eloquent and sensible: *Sharing Responsibility*, about how schools could become more democratic in their impact on the pupils' development, and *A Sense of Belonging*, about how schools should help young people through difficulties in their home situations and personal circumstances. A resource pack, *Climate for Learning*, provided materials for use in schools. A whole series of publications was issued under the general title of *Perspectives on Values in Education*. In truth it should be conceded that the SCCC staff were doing much to promote the main purposes of the Foundation. They were giving teachers opportunities to reflect upon the values that loomed large in the teaching of personal morality: notions of responsibility, cooperation, compassion and integrity were implicit in the documentation, and the seminars and conferences they organised encouraged serious thinking about the moral tasks facing modern teachers. They were unable, however, to provide guidance and experience in the knowledge and skills essential for moral teaching. It was apparent that this kind of competence was not then thought to be either necessary or possible to provide.

The trustees, in the meantime, were busy responding to numerous requests for funding for a wide range of projects, many of which could not be regarded as remotely relevant; even some of the projects we decided to fund were actually marginal to the requirements of Victor's trust deed. But we were able to set up a considerable number of projects and activities which materially furthered our own central priorities. The programmes we had initiated in St Andrew's College, Northern College and Moray

House had reached a stage of maturity at which they were able to influence teachers in primary and secondary schools, and many schools throughout Scotland were embarking on different forms of values education. We set up and fully funded a research project with the Scottish Council for Research in Education (SCRE) which enquired into the perception of values and their relevance in primary school teaching: the report, *Understanding Values Education in the Primary School* (1995) was comprehensive and influential. The research team undertook in-depth studies of values education in five primary schools, conducted a large postal survey to explore the issues emerging from the case studies and produced an analysis of their findings which far surpassed anything that had been done hitherto in the UK. Their findings were important but clearly suggested that we had a very long way to go. Parents had little information about the values being conveyed in school, and teachers agreed with parents that the ultimate responsibility for pupils' development of values lay with the home. It appeared that many teachers felt that the home carried the *only* responsibility. Teachers' perceptions of the values they taught were 'expressed in rather broad, overlapping terms', and although both heads and their staff regarded values education as a function of their schools, the methods they employed for fostering values were not clearly specified.

In order to extend the scope of our work in fulfilling Victor's ambitions we set up a major study of Values in the Nursery School, conducted by the University of Paisley; interestingly, the director of the project, Chris Holligan, was a young psychologist who had stayed with Victor in Countesswells House while he was a student, and had retained a great respect for the man and his work. We also sponsored an international conference of psychologists who worked in the field of child development and were interested in values and dispositions in infancy; the organiser, Colwyn Trevarthen of Edinburgh University, had a world-wide reputation for his researches into babies' socio-moral development, and his colleagueship proved greatly beneficial to us. When we funded a programme of enquiry into values education in the further education field, which resulted in the publication of a book, *Values in Further Education* (1998) edited by the philosopher John Halliday, we had covered a wide educational spectrum. We went further: we initiated and funded two major studies of values education in community education, one in Scotland by the Scottish Council for Community Education (now Community Scotland), and one in England and Wales undertaken by the Citizenship Foundation. Both had (and still have) a strong impact in the field of youth education.

In 1996–7 we decided to obtain an evaluation of our work as a Foundation, and commissioned Bridget Somekh of SCRE to do the work; she and her assistant, Michael Byrne, produced a report in 1997 entitled *The Gordon Cook Foundation Quinquennial Review*. It was a far-ranging study in depth of all that we had done since Victor's death. We were surprised by some of the findings. For example, it emerged that we had distributed funds in seven different categories: Research only (16 per cent), Development only (30 per cent), Research and Development (46 per cent), Advisory (1 per cent), Conferences (2 per cent), Networking (2 per cent), Dissemination (3 per cent). As they said, 'the Foundation is clear in its expectation that "research projects [should] have a strong applied element"', hence 83 per cent of the research funding had been for Applied or Action Research and 17 per cent for Theoretical Research. Most of our funding was directed towards the formal educational sectors, and the main targets were primary and secondary schooling. At that time, relatively little funding had gone to higher education (£43,000), pre-school (£25,000), youth work (£13,000) or further education (£10,000). On the whole, our funding since 1997 has continued these priorities, though (as I make clear below) we have undertaken some major new projects during the last few years.

The Somekh review also pointed out that the distribution of our funding had not been evenly spread throughout the UK. Since then, however, we have funded major projects in England and in Northern Ireland, and initiated and sponsored a number of UK-wide conferences. In 1996 we set up a project on 'Values Education in Northern Ireland' with Professor Alan Smith of the University of Ulster. We decided to assign a sum of £150,000 over three years, but in the event the project assumed major proportions and continued until the year 2000. This decision was called into question by our lawyers, who pointed out that Victor Cook's will had stated that the Foundation's remit should apply 'to England and Wales as well as Scotland', omitting mention of Northern Ireland, so that strictly speaking we had no powers to give funds for projects outside these countries. We decided that that had been a mere oversight on Victor's part; he would certainly not have wished to omit Northern Ireland; in any case we had legal powers to donate funds to any project 'abroad' that would be to the benefit of education 'at home'. In the event this was one of the most successful projects the Foundation ever undertook: values education proved hugely interesting and relevant in Northern Ireland and our initial activities developed into a big and politically important programme of development. We also funded a major project with the

Norham Foundation, represented by David Ingram. This project, Schools and Values, illustrated the effect of concentrating resources on a single school complex under the direction of a knowledgeable and committed moral philosopher: the Leicestershire schools involved became treasuries of knowledge and innovation in the simple processes of discussion of the impact of moral thinking in classroom learning.

In our desire to spread our largesse and our influence more widely we gave donations to a number of agencies which existed to further the role of values education in the UK: these included NAVET (National Association for Values in Education and Training), the secretary of which had left us an entertaining account of his visit to Victor Cook in the late 1980s (see pp. 97–8); the Centre for Citizenship Studies at Leicester University, which disseminated a values education broadsheet funded by the GCF to all secondary schools in England; and we were largely instrumental in setting up the Values Education Council (VEC), which brought together most of the organisations interested in values education, and which is still powerfully influential. We also initiated a scheme of grants to allow directors of education and head teachers to attend international conferences abroad, in particular those of the AME (Association for Moral Education) and the Character Education Forum, both of which were giving education for character and morality great prestige in the USA and throughout the world.

In June 1995 we commissioned a special feature in the *Times Educational Supplement*. The editor, Willis Pickard, a shrewd observer of the educational scene in Scotland, wrote a leading article describing the Foundation and its purposes, and mentioned some of our achievements. David Ingram, director of our project in Leicestershire, Schools and Values, offered an account of the Just School movement inspired by Lawrence Kohlberg in America, and put this in the context of an informative discussion of how in his area a group of schools had been developing a whole-school approach to values education. Monica Taylor of the National Foundation for Educational Research, one of the most distinguished leaders in moral educational research in the world, wrote about the establishment of the Values Educational Council which had been initiated with the financial and collegial assistance of the GCF. Margaret Johnstone, of Moray House Institute of Education (now the Education faculty of Edinburgh University) described the important study of values teaching in primary schools which had been undertaken for the GCF by her and colleagues Pamela Munn and Mairi-Ann Cullen, and introduced the survey of teachers' values directed by Janet Powney and colleagues in

SCRE. The feature included a list of 13 organisations currently engaged in some aspects of values education in the UK.

Two major initiatives which had important consequences for the work of the Foundation deserve mention, not only because they illustrate some ways in which our efforts were being directed but also because they had long-term repercussions in the history of values education. After I had attended a conference of the Association for Moral Education in Toronto, I arranged a year-long consultancy in Scotland for Professor Marvin Berkowitz. I had been deeply impressed by a workshop he conducted in the design and conduct of a moral reasoning programme for school students, and I invited him to come to Scotland to assist the Foundation. He came with his wife and son and soon made a strong and pleasant impact on the educational scene. He presented lectures and seminars at the teacher training institutes, attended many consultative meetings, wrote papers, introduced a wide range of educationists to the ideas and techniques of moral education in the USA, and gave our work a prestige and significance we had never achieved before. The other development was the setting up of a series of conferences held under the aegis of the Foundation.

The reports of these annual conferences – held each year from 1995 to 1999 – now constitute a treasure trove of papers giving accounts of the thinking that was going on in these years; they also recount the gradual development of maturity in thinking about values education, in Scotland and elsewhere in the UK, which has culminated in the present-day universal acceptance of its importance. The 1995 conference portrayed some uncertainty about the nature of values education. Ian Barr aired again the SCCC's nervousness about the possibility that the subject might be assigned a specific timetabled place in the formal curriculum. Willis Pickard observed that in his experience no one was seriously suggesting that values education should be a separate subject, and anyway teachers would not wish to add another slot in an already overcrowded curriculum, but they would certainly welcome more classroom materials and guidance on how to use them. Jim Conroy, director of the seminal St Andrew's College project on values education in the primary school, agreed that teachers did not want 'new discrete elements' or 'anything that might be deemed a frilly extra or as playing around the fringes of real education', but he urged us to continue to work on producing materials to help teachers come to terms with the clamant need to integrate values education in the life and work of the schools. Monica Taylor reminded participants that in England the 1988 Education Reform Act had required schools to offer a curriculum which includes teaching to promote the spiritual, moral and cultural development of pupils, and the erstwhile National Curriculum Council (now the Qualifications and Curriculum Authority) (QCA) was producing guidance documents on citizenship and moral development. She pleaded for schools to 'map' the values in their curricula, to work with pupils and parents on identifying the basic values they wish to promote and agree to cooperate to prosecute them; and she emphasised the salient need in our society to deal educationally with a range of moral issues occupying the space and time of the media. Marvin Berkowitz presented a long, complex and (for our purposes) highly appropriate paper, *A Perspective from Across the Pond*. As a research psychologist, working on the psychological processes of human development, and particularly on 'socio-moral reasoning', he had spent two years as a postdoctoral fellow studying under Kohlberg and had concentrated latterly on training educators in moral dilemma discussions and on the establishment of Just Community schools. It was his expertise in promoting moral reasoning development that had led the GCF to invite him to spend his sabbatical in Scotland, but we were also hoping that he would share with his Scottish colleagues his vast experience in the theory and practices of a variety of forms of moral education currently prevalent in the USA. He argued in favour of a 'grand theory' of moral education (the term he and the majority of American experts felt was the best overall conceptual indicator of the field) because there had been so many models created which ignored the 'fundamental nature of child development', which failed to distinguish between morality and related domains, and which propagated 'a misguided ethic' (such as relativism). He was aware that there was a 'plethora' of terms for this domain of education: moral education, values education, social education, character education, civic education, citizenship education, democratic education and so on.

Commenting on the work he had seen in the five months he had so far spent in Scotland, Berkowitz said that most of what he had seen was 'atheoretical': 'there seems to be neither a theory of human development nor a theory of education underpinning the curricula that are written for moral education programmes.' He noted that the Scottish Office Education Department's 1992 report on Religious and Moral Education 5–14 acknowledged a problem at the interface of religion and morality, that it was 'undoubtedly true' that 'one could not be religious without being concerned with morality', but it is also possible to show moral concern and a commitment without necessarily basing those on a religious life. His own view, representative of American views generally, was that 'religion has parts that are moral and parts that are social-conventional';

but he was clearly unable to recognise that Scots educators were on the whole not seriously exercised by the distinctions. During his period of work in Scotland he had found a 'profound lack of training in moral education for future teachers: they have not been exposed to the major models of moral education and they have not acquired the skills of moral education'. That was in 1995; the situation has not materially changed. One of our crucial needs today is to devise the means to give teachers, both during initial training and in continuous professional development, some knowledge of moral theory and the accompanying training in moral discussion management.

The editor of the 1995 report, Alex Rodger, has himself done much to provide practising teachers with insights into the nature of morality and the ways in which it can be applied in the classroom and elsewhere in the life of the school. His work for the GCF, on the Values Education Project, has produced valuable materials and guidance, and his own publications, such as *Developing Moral Community in a Pluralist School* (1996) provide excellent philosophical and pedagogical support for school development. The report of the 1996 conference continued the campaign to bring teachers up to date with modern thinking about values and their place in schooling, but it also offered 'fruitful dialogue' with related fields such as law and political theory. The report of the 1997 conference brought a new dimension of social concern to the scene. This was ably summarised by David Carr in his Introduction:

Briefly, one might identify three main distinguishable but related considerations behind current concern. The first reflects a degree of public panic at what is widely regarded as the breakdown of traditional mores under the influence of liberal individualism and economic consumerism; this is thought to be generally evident in a decline of discipline among the young – exhibited in the drug or crime oriented hedonism of this or that youth culture – but it has been highlighted for many by a number of deplorable, if more sporadic, recent outbursts of individual murder and mayhem. A second related reason, however, seems more expressive of a professional concern that recent politically-driven educational reforms have focused more on the economic than the moral benefits of education: that recent emphases on raising standards have been upon the academic or vocational goals of schooling to the serious neglect of more fundamental humanising concerns.

The keynote address by Dr Nicholas Tate, Chief Executive of the School

Curriculum and Assessment Authority (SCAA), dwelt squarely on the need for 'education for moral preparation' – a reaction against a period when 'anything that was not a subject, or could not be tested, fell under suspicion of being "soft"'. He described the work of the National Forum on Values in Education and the Community which had been set up to identify the values held in common by its 150 members and to recommend ways in which moral education in schools might better be supported. The Forum had achieved a surprising degree of consensus which was reinforced by a 'technically robust' national consultation with parents, teachers and the general public. It found a broad support for a wide range of values (with inevitable disagreement on the sources of these values and on their application to particular circumstances) and it recommended that the shared values it identified be used as a starting point for the work of schools and for 'efforts by the rest of society to support schools in these aspects of their role'. SCAA accepted the Forum's recommendation and was seeking government support for 'a national push on values education in schools'. Dr Tate argued strenuously for 'explicit provision for moral education in the overt schools curriculum'. In this he was re-echoing the plea put forward in the SCCC's *Values in Education* document of 1991; but his initiative was overtaken by the election of a New Labour government and its prompt action in setting up the mechanisms for a new drive to establish education in citizenship. The Foundation's conferences in 1998 and 1999 were both devoted to education in 'values and citizenship' – a term now used officially in all the four nations of the UK. Education for citizenship, the principal goal sought by Victor Cook in his lifetime and the main requirement of his legacy to his trustees, now seemed at last to have been given the imprimatur of government at all levels.

Chapter Fourteen

New emphases: values education for health and enterprise

U nder the chairmanship of Peter Clarke and David Adams we began to exercise more methodical ways of selecting projects and overseeing our funding. We decided to identify a number of issues and projects, giving priority to major, long-term programmes of development. Accordingly in 1999 we adopted in principle a short list of projects which would address the central interests of the Foundation. This included an extension of our sponsorship of conferences, extending both our 'geographical' coverage and the range of participants we invited. From this policy emerged the 'Four Nations Conferences' – which brought together, entirely at our expense, persons interested in values education and working in the field in England, Northern Ireland, Scotland and Wales. This was one of the most successful ventures the Foundation had ever undertaken, as it achieved a general affirmation that values education, in its widest sense, lies at the heart of education for citizenship. It is true to say that, in the six conferences we held between 1988 and 2003, all devoted to various aspects of education for citizenship, all the most important organisations in that field were brought into contact with each other and with the Foundation. Our activity predated the official governmental initiatives, and it was generally welcomed. We formed new links with the Institute for Global Ethics UK Trust which gave us a productive relationship with the main players in the four constituent nations of Britain: they also brought us into contact with the IGE (US), the parent body based in Camden, Maine. The Chief Executive of IGE (UK), Sheila Bloom, soon became a major adviser and assistant to the Foundation, arranging meetings for us, running consultations, suggesting new strategies for furthering our ideas, and introducing us to a wide variety of leading professionals in such areas as law, the media, the civil services, and the world of commerce. It was Sheila who brought us together with the trustees of the Comino Foundation. Dmitri Comino was (in some ways very like Victor Cook) a successful industrialist who had decided to devote his considerable wealth to enhancing the commercial, manufacturing and educational competences of the nation. Among other fruitful instances of our cooperation was a series of consultations, still ongoing, held under the joint aegis of the two foundations and convened by Sheila Bloom; held in the gracious ambience of Windsor Castle, these meetings bring people together from various spheres to discuss such topics as human rights, the responsibilities which are intrinsic to good citizenship, and the problems inherent in transforming values cultures in society. Through Sheila, too, we have formed a creative relationship with the founder of IGE, Rushworth Kidder (one of the most influential moral educators in America) and his numerous associates.

Another major initiative we took in the last years of the twentieth century was a collaborative programme of values education with police authorities. With our help the Grampian Police Service set up a team to produce guidance and teaching materials dealing with aspects of health education and personal development: a 'Police Box' containing materials was marketed and taken up by police authorities throughout Britain, enabling police authorities to work with teachers in schools on courses providing information and advice to children on the many problems confronting them in relation to smoking, drugs, sex and other aspects of modern life which cause young people to deviate from normal desirable behaviour. This venture was particularly satisfying to us because it went some way to meet one of Victor Cook's main requests, that we should further the cause of health education. In pursuit of this general objective we also offered a substantial grant to the Health Education Board of Scotland (HEBS) to strengthen their educational work.

Neither of these projects went near to meeting one of the most prominent of Victor Cook's ambitions in respect of health education. As we have seen (in Chapter 2) he was an early advocate of educating children in healthy eating. Despite the good efforts of various organisations devoted to providing guidance on diet to schools and youth organisations, it remains apparent that despite the fears voiced decades ago by people like Victor Cook and Doris Grant too many of our youngsters – and, it has to be said, their elders – eat unhealthy junk food to the detriment of their physical wellbeing. Many schools try to counteract the propaganda of the fast food industry, discouraging the sale of unhealthy foodstuffs and encouraging the pupils to eat fruit and plain fare instead of excessive salt, sugars and fat. To make a real difference, however, it is not enough to preach the virtues of healthy eating and provide materials to teachers. Schools need to give high priority to the study of personal health and the values involved – the negative values of the marketplace and the positive values that promote wise nutrition and exercise. Values education has a central role to play in the improvement of personal wellbeing; as for other aspects of values education, this ought to be recognised as a whole-school responsibility. There are curriculum guidelines and materials for physical education teachers, demonstrating the value of good diets for prowess in games and sports, and there are courses available in the USA which point up the values of working to succeed in athletics and team games – the making of 'heroes' who are role models of fair play, leadership and care for others as well as the more conventional image of success in the field. One of our future objectives in the Foundation should be the development of values-driven work in sport.

In keeping with our policy of creating links with a wider range of bodies concerned with values we set up a project on 'Professional Ethics'. We commissioned Dr Ivor Sutherland, formerly Registrar of the General Teaching Council for Scotland (GTC), who had a long acquaintanceship with matters arising from professional and ethical problems, to bring together a group of representatives of various professions to study the nature of professional ethics and the best ways they can be applied. The assembled group varied in their origins but were at one in their interest in the subject: they spoke with authority, as they represented senior ranks in law, police service, social work, medicine and education. They formed links also with similar projects in the Royal Society of Arts (RSA) and Bristol University. A conference was held in the spring of 2003, and the subsequent publication aroused wide interest. Another conference held in March 2004 extended the sphere of interest in professional ethics. Ethics are of course essential to professional integrity, and the moral issues which arise in the course of any professional person's everyday work generate a profusion of problems which are best dealt with in the context of some form of training which can be recognised as 'values education' for the practitioners.

A major development in our work at this time was a renewed interest in education in the values related to work and business, enterprise and entrepreneurship. We had earlier given a donation to a body called the Industrial Society (now the Work Foundation) which included in its activities the mounting of seminars for senior pupils to provide them with information on modern business and industry, and crucially the importance of economic progress and the conditions needed for improving it. As individuals, some of the trustees had been involved in national efforts to raise awareness in schools of the importance of industrial and commercial enterprise. Charles Skene had been much involved with the programme of activities initiated by the national Industry Year 1986. As chairman of the Scottish Vocational Education Council (SCOTVEC),

Peter Clarke was a key figure in the reforms which led to a great improvement in the provision of education and training in crafts and industrial occupations. I was myself an active agent in the development of TVEI (Technical and Vocational Education Initiative) in the schools. Bart McGettrick and David Adams, as principals of teacher training institutions, were responsible for important new courses designed to give future teachers a better understanding of business and industry. The values dimension of the new emphasis on work was explored by a committee of which I was a member, called 'Education for the Industrial Society', and our publication, *An Education for Life and Work* (1983), set out to show how the whole school should contribute to giving students a fresh understanding of the values of work, business, commerce and industry, and how every area of the curriculum could be made to connect with the world of wealth creation. In 1993 the Foundation was associated with a consultation between representatives of business and education, arranged by Varry Pugh, director in Scotland of Understanding British Industry, Allison Long of Heriot-Watt University, and myself. We set out to try to answer the following questions: What do business people think of schools? Is 'value for money' a fair demand? Is school management sufficiently business-like? How can people from industry and commerce best help our schools? How can schools best help our economic progress? While there could be no realistic expectation that our answers could be definitive, we were pleased and encouraged by the degree of consensus achieved. It was generally accepted that schools need to learn from successful business management how they can develop higher staff morale and commitment to the purposes of the enterprise, a result in some measure of encouraging people to value themselves, their work, and their contribution to the welfare of society. It was agreed that the widespread suspicion among educators in schools and universities that there was some kind of conspiracy to impose 'business values' ought to be confronted by rational discussion and the frank exchange of information and views in conferences among the different constituencies in the community. There were genuine benefits to be derived from adapting modern management techniques to the running of schools and colleges. It was agreed that recent political calls for 'more value for money' derived from genuine anxieties about how limited public resources could be better deployed to achieve more effective education and training: since as a nation we were increasingly forced to compete with others to produce more attractive goods and services we needed to raise our standards of production and marketing, and that meant raising the efficiency of our education services.

(Some years later, the GCF collaborated with the Quality Scotland
Foundation in the production of a 'Management Framework for School
Excellence'. This was an adaptation done by a group of senior teachers and
business people, brought together by Ian Dale of Quality Scotland and
myself, of the European Foundation for Quality Management guidelines
on 'facilitated assessment' for chief executives. This proved to be an excellent
tool for school self-assessment, much commended by HM Inspectors of
Education.) The report of the conference, which I edited and disseminated
with the title of *Values Compared*, was soon out of print. The participants
included Ian Matheson of the Clydesdale Bank, Ron Lander, a pioneer of
business-education liaison, Tony McLaren of Digital Equipment Scotland
(DEC) (*sic*), Tony Fitzpatrick of British Petroleum and a number of distinguished educationists including Douglas Osler, HM Senior Chief Inspector,
Lesley Kydd of the Open University, Professors Gordon Milne and Margaret
Sutherland, Colin Finlayson, head teacher of James Gillespies High School,
Edinburgh, and Lindsay Roy of Inverkeithing High School; no fewer than
four of the GCF trustees attended, and several of these participants
welcomed this introduction to the concerns of the GCF and remained
true friends of the Foundation.

DEC had developed a business game for schools, youth training groups,
further education college students and voluntary groups of teachers, and
earlier in 1993 I had been invited by Moray House staff to evaluate the
game as it was played over three days by graduate students; this was with
a view to its being utilised as an element in teacher training. My report
reiterated the view that in the modern world the welfare of our culture,
as well as our material prosperity, depends to a significant extent on the
success of the commercial and industrial enterprises in which people
earned their living: 'whether big or small, business matters to everyone –
but during the last quarter century businesses have realised that people
matter to them.' The game, called 'DEChallenge' (pronounced *deck
challenge*), set out to give students a positive understanding of how business operates. Positive attitudes combine with educational and technical
skills to develop business potential, and there is an important association
here with values education. Self-development includes the ability to accept
responsibility, readiness to change and willingness to cooperate. To the
basic skills of literacy and numeracy we must add the less easily discernible
skills such as the ability to adapt to new circumstances, to be able to
work in teams, to learn new methods, to perceive new opportunities; and
above all self-development must inspire the motivation to work hard
and persevere even in the face of apparent failure. I reached the firm

conclusion that it was highly beneficial to the training of teachers to give them this kind of experience.

During the last ten years the world of business has become increasingly willing to help schools to produce young people with higher competencies for work. Values education occupies an important place in these efforts, though – whether because they are not aware of the educational import of what they are doing, or because neither teachers nor business people are fully persuaded that values education can produce worthwhile results – there has been too little interest in the development of the values and attitudes that underlie and strengthen young people's commitment to work; technical abilities are important, of course, but they are not enough. Enterprising behaviour needs to be studied and methods developed for nurturing the attributes that generate it. This subject formed part of the agenda for the GCF 1996 conference, 'Changing Contexts for Values Education'. Of particular interest was Professor Russell Keat's paper on *Values and the Enterprise Culture*. Russell Keat was Professor of Political Theory at Edinburgh University, and he had been working on the values of the enterprise culture for several years. He reminded us that advocates of enterprise education regard it as essential to the 'maximally effective operation of the market system'. According to this view, notoriously expounded by Lord Young, a key figure in the drive for economic progress in the Thatcher government, economic success requires the 'right kinds of individuals' – enterprising individuals – with appropriate types of motivation, attitudes and self-understanding. Enterprising qualities are thought, moreover, to be intrinsically valuable – morally desirable characteristics which underlie an admirable way of life. This view can be contrasted, Keat argued, with the belief (put forward initially by Adam Smith) that a market system is in itself beneficent, by its very working, even if it relies on each individual acting from mere self-interest and even if some are motivated only by greed, acquisitiveness or vanity: there is no need for educational intervention – the market should be left alone to do its work. But proponents of enterprise education insist that enterprising individuals can and should be helped to develop by appropriate teaching and guided experience.

Enterprising persons, it has been shown, are autonomous, self-reliant, able to take responsibility for their own lives, and to make their own decisions. Thus when things go wrong they do not assume there is always someone else to blame, or someone whose job it is to put things right. They are polar opposites to those who are supposedly mired in the 'culture of dependency'. Enterprising individuals display high levels of energy, optimism and initiative. They do not hang back and wait to see what others will do before committing themselves to action. But this ideal picture of the enterprising self has three major defects, explained Keat. Firstly, it fails to take account of the extent to which any individual will be dependent on others. Many of the most beneficial enterprises undertaken by human beings rely upon cooperation and collective effort, and every enterprising person will only be able to accomplish anything by means of the help of others, no matter how independent he or she may feel. Secondly, there is a tendency for advocates of enterprising activity to neglect the moral restraints that human beings depend on: that is, we cannot admire such people as drug dealers or traffickers in enslaved prostitutes, no matter how enterprising they are. The enterprising person may confuse the pursuit of opportunities with mere opportunism. Thirdly, it is false to claim that the effectiveness of a market economy depends mainly on the work of enterprising individuals: most economic production relies upon collective endeavour, and the qualities which make for successful business, such as cooperation, reciprocity, willingness to subordinate one's own interest to those of the team, are often wholly different from the qualities commended in the enterprising person.

The pros and cons of these arguments form the substance of many lively discussions in staffrooms, study groups and coffee lounges. The GCF trustees have debated them over many years around the dinner table – and we still do. It is one of our strengths as a group that we can take sides with passion – and considerable glee – and still buckle down to our main tasks. In the Foundation the great proponent of enterprise and entrepreneurship is Charles Skene, who has exercised a remarkable influence on his colleagues in various circles, and on the educational community at large. His own life story is a record of enterprise, energy, courage and perseverance. Having left school at the age of sixteen, he joined the sixty-seven-year-old family photography business, and within a few years he built it into one of the largest and most profitable in the UK. He never lost his interest in the profession and he is still a distinguished figure in the world of photographic arts. But by his late thirties he had diversified his business interests and become the largest owner of residential property in Aberdeen and one of the largest in Glasgow. In his forties he added a flourishing removals business to his company, and in the 1980s and 1990s he built up enterprises in retirement housing, nursing homes, serviced offices and business centres. In the course of this hectic career he found time to serve his community, founding the Aberdeen Civic Society; he became a sponsor of the arts, creating an award for the most outstanding young musician at the annual Aberdeen International Youth Festival. In his businesses he exhibits his care for the disabled by employing disabled youngsters.

Outside business Charles's main preoccupation has been the promotion of enterprise education. Like so many successful business persons, he has long believed that our economic progress can be improved only by changing the way in which we educate our young people: we must make them understand the economic facts of life; develop their ability to be enterprising; awaken any latent gift of entrepreneurial talents; inculcate them with the belief that they can succeed in their chosen career if they are sufficiently determined. An archetypal Scottish lad o' pairts, he attributes his success to hard work and implacable determination rather than to any natural genius or sheer luck – 'if I can do it anybody can.' But unlike many busy businessmen, Charles Skene has devoted a great deal of his time to translating his beliefs into action. As an active leader in the Scottish Chambers of Commerce, he organised meetings at which economic problems were discussed and solutions proposed; he associated himself with the Royal Society of Arts (RSA) and the Confederation of British Industry (CBI) to counter by education what was believed to be an 'anti-industry culture' by mounting, as part of the Industry Year 1986 programme, careers fairs and young people's conventions to tell them about industry and commerce as potential goals for satisfying and profitable careers. In 1987 he launched the Skene Young Entrepreneurs Award scheme, its object being to 'encourage an enterprising culture in primary and secondary schools in Scotland and to reward success'. Sixteen years later, this is still an outstandingly successful educational programme, inspiring both teachers and pupils to explore ways of conducting business by setting up 'mini-companies', selecting products, organising themselves to take responsibility for various administrative functions, studying problems of costing and production, and engaging in all the tasks of communicating, negotiating, buying materials and making and selling finished goods or services. Quite apart from the opportunities the scheme gives teachers to strengthen basic skills, it provides hours of enjoyable activity (and work that has to be done for deferred gratification) and offers a unique method of developing the values and attitudes which are most desirable in enterprising behaviour: appreciation of opportunities to profit from your labour, the need to take risks, to assume and manage personal responsibility, to sacrifice immediate pleasure for the promise of rewards to be won after sustained effort; and an understanding of how transactions – the giving and taking, the getting and spending, the keeping of promises – are integral to a satisfying and productive life.

Charles Skene also devoted a great deal of time and effort to lobbying the appropriate authorities on the subject of enterprise education. As a result of his powerful argumentation – he can write with authority and punch on the subject – he was invited to become Visiting Professor of Entrepreneurship at Robert Gordon University in Aberdeen. His friends and colleagues greeted this appointment with some amusement: he had long scoffed at the futility of academic research and exposition – and he met our teasing with characteristic good humour and retaliation. In 2002 he endowed the chair of entrepreneurship at the university, and they renamed their Centre of Entrepreneurship in his honour. When the Scottish Executive decided to set up a review group on 'Enterprise and Lifelong Learning' he accepted an invitation to become a member, and he took a leading part in their deliberations; as might be expected they produced a short and forceful set of recommendations, couched in language that typified Charles's own style. With much satisfaction he told his friends that, unlike most reports, this one includes many 'musts' and not the more usual 'shoulds'. The title also reflected Charles's personality: *Determined to Succeed*. The group, ably chaired by Nicol Stephen, MSP, insisted in their report that every pupil from P1 to P6 must have an entitlement to enterprise activities on an annual basis, and in addition pupils in S5 and S6 should have 'an entitlement to case studies based on local or Scottish businesses'. Business organisations must identify 'champions' to work with a 'Ministerial Strategic Forum'; resources must be provided for 'appropriate experiential entrepreneurial activities' in all schools. Enterprise development officers must be appointed and 'strategic partnerships' arranged to engage with local business and organisations to further the provision of enterprise education. There must be 'a major expansion in the involvement of businesses in our schools', and a National Award scheme set up to build on current schemes. There must be more provision of guidance, support materials and careers information. Research must be undertaken into part-time work done by young people while at school. The Scottish Qualifications Authority (SQA) and Learning and Teaching Scotland (LTS) must work with business organisations to 'review and improve the provision of Enterprise in Education within the framework of National Qualifications'. Teacher training must be developed. Monitoring and evaluation must be provided to ensure that the recommendations will be implemented and developed. In order to further this work, the GCF donated funds to the National Centre for Enterprise Education to meet some of the cost of a development officer.

As with most of the injunctions levelled at educators by business people, the central difficulty that ensues is the absence of pedagogical knowledge and expertise. It is easy to approve the sentiments and aspirations they put forward, but teachers are often at a loss as to how they can be turned into practical, everyday instruction, since the 'skills' and 'attitudes' which seem to be required are undefined and teaching procedures have not been devised and structured. This is not to say that the curricular and pedagogical implications cannot be developed, given the required resources. The 'mini-company' programme has earned credibility and endorsement from many teachers, but it is still an 'add-on', occasional project; 'case studies' can provide inspiration, and real business projects for older students can offer guidance and practical experience, but these too tend to be seen rather as ancillary activities. On the other hand, much can be done in schools about what Charles has called 'our anti-enterprise, risk-averse culture': that would involve values education combined with the kind of inspirational effects expected from case studies of successful careers and enterprises. What is needed is research and experimentation of different kinds, to build up a corpus of theory, praxis and guidance on the basis of which teachers can design and try out procedures and materials. *Determined to Succeed* is an adequate starting point, if the education systems accepts it as such. That brings us back to values. Too many teachers dismiss enterprise education as another questionable innovation. A *Times Educational Supplement* critique of the report pointed out that although 'pupils must be made keenly aware of the world of work as well as their own potential to contribute to it' that will not necessarily be achieved by 'ramming enterprise education down their throats, or symbolically promoting budding entrepreneurs at the expense of those less gifted in that direction'. Charles Skene's riposte in the same journal was brisk:

Entitlement to enterprise education for all will produce, hopefully, a few entrepreneurial stars and many, many more enterprising Scots. It will also increase the self-confidence, creativity, flexibility and leadership skills of all pupils whether they go into professions, academia, health-care, the trades, or self-employment. A win-win situation for Scotland.

This was well said. No one would erect the entrepreneur into a pattern for all members of society; but to want to increase the number of 'stars' our schools and colleges produce is surely a worthwhile aspiration. And to aim at improving the potential of all to be more enterprising is a sensible and achievable goal.

It is not the case that enterprising individuals are bound to be self-centred and ruthless: many of the most successful entrepreneurs in business have combined their determination to succeed in worldly terms with a measure of social and personal altruism that is well above the average. There is no such thing as the perfect theoretical model of personality; we are all mixtures. Educators who embrace the drive towards more effective enterprise for our society will also aim at developing the means to produce more enterprising young people: that will require the inclusion of values education in the work of the school.

Chapter Fifteen

Education for citizenship

Foremost among our priorities in the 1990s was education for citizenship. It has been widely acknowledged that we were playing a leading part in the development of the subject many years before it became topical. In the 1988 Education Act for England and Wales citizenship was commended as a cross-curricular theme but there was no official requirement that it should have a place in the formal curriculum. This was understandable, as there was little educational interest in the subject: there was no recognised definition of the term, nor was there much effort to design pedagogical structures or materials. Among politicians, however, there was an increasing anxiety about the evident cynicism among the public in respect of the work of government, particularly among the young; and this manifested itself in low voter turnouts at elections. In 1990 a Speaker's Commission report, *Encouraging Citizenship*, gave a stimulus to academics and others to make arrangements for research and development. I had long been an advocate of citizenship education, mainly through my association as an HMI with the subject of Modern Studies; but this was only to be found in Scotland, and it had become merely an option in the examination menu in secondary schools; and although teachers and inspectors wanted a greater element of values study in the subject the predominance of the examination syllabus tended to restrict attention rather to 'civics', the study of governance and its structures. Nevertheless the existence of Modern Studies gave people the impression, both in Scotland and elsewhere, that 'citizenship' was being taught in Scotland. As a response to the invitation in the Speaker's Commission report, the University of Leicester set up a Centre for Citizenship Studies in Education in its annexe in Northampton, under the direction of Professor Ken Fogelman, who was already an authority on the subject. I was an early visitor to the centre, and I arranged for the GCF to provide funds for the dissemination of teaching materials to schools throughout the UK. In the main the only schools interested in using these materials were primary schools and secondary departments catering for less academic pupils; but the number of materials that became available was high, the quality was excellent, and the number of teachers interested grew annually. Again, however, the materials tended to concentrate on the 'civics' side: values education in this regard was slow to gain the interest of teachers during the early years of the decade. The Foundation continued to do what it could to promote interest, and we were pleased to see the growth of other organisations such as the Citizenship Foundation, based in London and supported by an impressive array of political and academic figures.

At the GCF conference of 1991 my paper, *On Character and Citizenship: The Gordon Cook Foundation's Policies*, made it clear that we were enthusiastic about the teaching of 'social values' and 'the attributes of the good citizen':

> An experiential education in citizenship will comprise a great variety of responsibilities ranging through the whole age spectrum: primary pupils helping to look after the young ones; helping to keep the school tidy; helping to plan or organise school or class events; secondary pupils running their own mini-companies, participating in class, year or school councils, helping to draw up rules of conduct and appearance; meeting and questioning community and social leaders: such activities should not be random or incidental, but integrated in a carefully designed values education curriculum which inhabits the whole curriculum matrix. For the Foundation, 'citizenship' connotes a range of competencies, dispositions and value positions which render an individual useful and creative in society.

Most of these sentiments and proposals were 'in the air' but not familiar everyday realities in schools. Official priorities for curriculum or professional training did not include citizenship education.

In England, where the Scottish Modern Studies curriculum was much admired, there was a strong desire to achieve a high measure of political education: this was not wholly due to the advent of a new Labour government, though there was a strong connection; there was all-party support for the proposal that educational goals should include the development of more civic awareness, and motivation among the young to enlarge their knowledge of how government works and how to express their personal aspirations in political terms. At the GCF 1998 conference, which produced the report *Values Education for Democracy and Citizenship*, the first keynote address was given by Bernard (now Sir Bernard) Crick, chair of the Advisory Group on Education for Citizenship set up by the new government soon after its inauguration. The all-party support for this initiative was indicated by its membership (which included Lord Baker, who had been the Conservative Secretary of State for Education) and the wide range of opinion consulted. The Crick Report, *Education for Citizenship and the Teaching of Democracy in Schools* (QCA 1998), exhibited a strong advocacy of citizenship as a training in social and political action. Expressing anxiety about 'the worrying levels of apathy, ignorance and cynicism about public life', a view prevalent especially among members of parliament, it recommended that citizenship education should be 'a statutory entitlement' in the curriculum and that all schools should be required to show they are fulfilling the obligations that this places upon them. It set out specific learning outcomes for each key stage and recommended that 'standards and objectivity' should be officially inspected. An Order issued by the Department for Education and Enterprise (DfEE) should declare that citizenship education in schools and colleges must include the 'knowledge, skills and values relevant to the nature and practices of participative democracy'. The new subject should be assigned five per cent of curriculum time, but schools should be free to combine elements with other subjects, and citizenship education should be related to 'whole school issues including school ethos, organisations and structures'.

The report is explicit about what the Group meant by 'effective education for citizenship':

> Firstly, children learning from the very beginning self-confidence and socially and morally responsible behaviour both in and beyond the classroom, both towards those in authority and towards each other... Secondly, learning about and becoming helpfully involved in the life and concerns of their communities, including learning through community involvement and service to the community... Thirdly, pupils learning about and how to make themselves effective in public life through knowledge, skills and values...

In his address to the GCF conference, Crick emphasised the moral dimension of citizenship education. Reiterating his Group's metaphor, 'three heads on one body', in which social and moral responsibility comes first, he suggested that this 'may be thought of as common ground (indeed for all education) or as the essential precondition for what is commonly thought of as citizenship both as teaching and practice'. The learning outcomes his report proposed were precise: (a) values, concepts and attitudes, (b) skills, and (c) knowledge.

It was not clear to many of us, however, what precisely was meant by 'social and moral responsibility'. The term might seem to be a pleonasm: is it possible to be morally responsible and not socially responsible? The Crick Group stated that they believed that guidance on moral values and personal development are essential preconditions of citizenship, but they did not explain how that should be done; they were confident that 'through learning and discussion, concepts of fairness, and attitudes to the law, to rules, to decision-making, to authority, to their local environment and social responsibility etc' children would acquire the requisite concepts and dispositions. No doubt the units set up by the government to provide guidance and materials to teachers of citizenship would meet this need – and in the event that has proved to be the case in large measure. The concept of 'political literacy' (a term first introduced by Bernard Crick in his book *In Defence of Politics* (1964)) was elaborated in another address by Richard Pring, Professor of Education at Oxford (and a longterm friend of the GCF). To be politically literate, he suggested, means that one has a grasp of the basic concepts through which one might understand the social world from a distinctly political point of view. The social world is 'sieved' through such concepts as 'power', 'authority', 'legal rights and obligations', 'government'. Educating children politically would be to give them an increasingly sophisticated grasp of those concepts through which we understand the distribution of power within society, and in particular the various ways in which that power and authority are exercised between government and governed. That understanding must embrace such basic moral concepts as 'justice' and 'fairness', 'rights' and 'obligations'. Political and social education lie essentially in developing those 'public concepts' we need to understand the world – not in fact giving or forming particular political beliefs:

> Only then can the young person be able to engage intelligently with the issues – follow the arguments, challenge conclusions in the light of evidence, see things from a different point of view, and develop an independent though reasoned and justified political perspective.

But the acquisition of those concepts is not enough, said Pring. Young people need to develop certain skills and attitudes, especially those skills and attitudes concerned with engagement in serious reflection and discussion:

> One might refer here to an interest in those issues which affect human wellbeing, justice and fairness, getting at the truth, openness to evidence

and reasoning. And such engagement does require skills, particularly the social skills in handling contrary arguments, in listening to alternative points of view, and in handling emotive responses to positions sincerely held.

Pring made it clear that he believed there was a need for the direct teaching of skills in reflection and discourse, and that this was feasible: he cited Bruner's argument that the 'key ideas' which structure the thinking in any discipline can be put across to any child at any age in an intellectually respectable form.

Richard Pring was adducing his arguments in favour of political education, for that conformed to his remit. But those of us who want moral education – or values education, to use the more fashionable term – to be given more time and pedagogical effort, believe that developing an understanding of moral concepts, and acquiring the skills of rational thinking, would in themselves be the best possible precondition for education in citizenship. In an interesting appendix to the Crick Report, Bernard writes to John Tomlinson, then the chair of the 'Passport Project', devoted to the promotion of personal and social education (PSE): 'Citizenship depends upon good behaviour and an ability to make informed moral judgements; but it is far more than that.' He was of course referring to the knowledge and meaningful experience that make up 'political literacy'; but the corollary is also true: citizenship requires political literacy, but it is far more than that. The good citizen behaves well and knows how government works, but also knows how to make informed and critical judgements about political issues and events.

At the GCF conference of 1999, on 'Education for Citizenship', shortly before the formal opening of the new Scottish parliament, the Deputy Minister for Children and Education, Peter Peacock, in an intelligent and well delivered opening address, evinced a strong desire for education in 'democracy' but showed little familiarity with the work on citizenship education that was going on throughout the UK. The keynote address by Douglas Osler, HMSCI (Her Majesty's Senior Chief Inspector of Schools) was a closely reasoned, well structured survey of factors likely to contribute to 'a pragmatic and practical definition of education for citizenship in Scotland'. He reminded us that throughout Europe, North America and the Pacific rim, education systems are reacting in similar ways to change in commerce, in culture and in social conditions. There is increasing concern to drive up educational standards, to provide longer and more effective schooling, to wrestle with issues of national identity and cultural diversity; and there is increasing interest in 'what schools are, and should be doing, to promote responsible citizenship and moral values'. Do schools, he asked, have a role in developing the values which are fundamental to good citizenship? His answer is reasoned but positive:

> There is certainly an expectation in most societies that schools do have some responsibility for cultural transfer, namely the collective memory and experience of earlier generations and the accepted social norms of the current society. But surely that must not imply a static or unquestioning role for schools. Most people's views of education vary significantly and are usually heavily conditioned by their own past experience. We have to look a little further ahead in considering the citizens we want to see emerging from our school system. We also have to acknowledge that schools must react to external forces for change – economic, social and political. The process of change is inevitable. There needs therefore to be a process by which the school develops young people capable of embracing such change; and indeed initiating change for the common good. If change is continuous, can we define universally accepted and constant values which must be transmitted through the school, or are we in an era of moral relativism where we define moral values simply in terms of how we would behave again without personal regret?

The aims of the GCF, he suggested, provide something of a way forward:

> To encourage young people to think about and make explicit their own values; to assess the appropriateness of these for their own and others' wellbeing; and to decide how to adopt other values which might enhance their own personal and social wellbeing.

He pointed out that the GCF explicitly declares its commitment to the development of a pluralistic society where social policy is based on public debate, and that we do not identify a single set of desirable values, but are willing to give, as examples, respect for the rule of law, honesty, tolerance, integrity, industriousness and kindliness.

Osler firmly endorsed these aims, and in particular the principle that young people need to be encouraged to develop their individual values and to recognise that these personal values must take into account accepted social mores and the needs of others. He reminded us that the teacher does not operate in a moral vacuum – he or she has a clear role in promoting positive values and beliefs, in informing by precept or by personal example the values of children to allow them to become valuable citizens. The conundrum for schools is to identify and encourage accepted social values and yet encourage critical thinking, debate, flexibility and independence of thought; to reflect what society values in its past and also influence how society will develop in the future. This was a fine portrayal of the classic liberal-traditional position commended by the philosopher David Carr (see Chapter 12) which combines respect for bygone wisdom but insists that our thinking and conclusions must develop in the light of fresh insights.

Similar positions had been taken by the SCCC and by speakers at the GCF conference in 1998. Henry Maitles of Strathclyde University, a leader in the training of teachers of Modern Studies, maintained that that subject claimed the development of positive values as a central aim. He reiterated an SCCC's statement that it should develop open-mindedness, tolerance and the moral and ethical responsibilities of individuals. And Donald Christie, in a wide-ranging paper on Citizenship Education in the primary school, cited Ralph Waldo Emerson's dictum that 'character is higher than intellect' in defending the assertion that in any curriculum designed to foster moral reasoning there must be an emphasis on action and not just on exercises designed to promote thought. The new perspective, said Christie, 'demands the integration of individual independence and personal morality on the one hand, with interdependence and social responsibility on the other'. If children are to learn to be good citizens they should be critically reflective, morally autonomous and socially active. There is a case for the teaching of 'basic skills' for citizenship: these might be (1) emotional awareness and sensitivity; (2) empathy; (3) pro-social behaviour; (4) understanding relationships: 'if we take sociomoral development and citizenship education seriously, why should we deny space within the curriculum for structured, stimulating, classroom activities to promote the relevant basic skills in this domain?'

Shortly after the 1999 GCF conference the SCCC published an important paper called *The School Curriculum and the Culture of Scotland*. This declared that the establishment of a Scottish parliament should be seen as a golden opportunity to create 'a new political culture in Scotland'. The outstanding feature of this new culture should be inclusiveness. All young people should have access to knowledge about the workings of the constitution and their own part in it; they should have a 'critical understanding' of law and order, finance, health and other features of government; understanding of government should be 'embedded in the curriculum'; teachers should aim 'to excite young people's enthusiasm, not for political institutions of government as such, but for the democratic processes of government at local, national, UK and European levels'. The curriculum should foster a sense of active and responsible citizenship, and equip young people with the capability to engage actively in issues arising in these and other fields. This is best achieved by including education for citizenship in the curriculum, and by encouraging young people to take responsible moral and ethical decisions in their personal and public lives. When the Scottish Executive decided to take an initiative in respect of citizenship education they naturally turned to Learning and Teaching Scotland (LTS) which had been established in July 2000 as a successor to the SCCC. The Advisory Council of LTS set up a Review Group to 'develop a view of the nature, importance and aims of education for citizenship from 3 to 18 and the characteristics of effective practice and to describe this succinctly'. The Review Group issued its first report in September 2000. Named *Education for Citizenship in Scotland: a Paper for Discussion and Consultation*, it rehearsed the sort of views about the aims and purposes of citizenship education which had been put forward in many contexts in recent years: although there was nothing exceptionable in it, it was inevitably brief, having been produced in haste, and it was in the form of a genuine consultation, with questions in the margins to frame people's responses. A preface by Professor Pamela Munn, who chaired the Group, makes it plain that the paper proposes only 'broad notions', and the aims and methodology indicated for the subject are indeed broad rehearsals of the current received wisdom about the provision of citizenship education. Although there is no depth of discussion in the paper, the preface blandly states that the Group had concluded 'that it is neither appropriate nor adequate to create a new subject that attempts to encompass "citizenship education"'. No doubt what was intended here was that the Group believed that schools should not allocate timetabled periods for citizenship education – in fact the subject had been created many years before in many places; and in proposing 'aims' and a rationale and learning outcomes the Group itself was according 'subject status' to it in a real sense. The inadequacy of this introductory paper mattered little, since it served mainly as a stimulus for many consultative meetings conducted by LTS staff throughout the country. It asked some relevant questions, and it provided opportunities for the consideration of the more important issues. In June 2002 LTS issued another publication, this time called *A Paper for Discussion and Development*. This went over the same ground as did the first paper, but with more detail and more authority. It also carried the imprimatur of a preface by the Minister for Education and Young People, Cathie Jamieson, and she endorsed its contents as 'the basis for a national framework for education and citizenship from 3 to 18'. Another preface, by Professor Tom Wilson, Chairman of LTS, made it clear that the subject was now a National Priority (called 'Values and Citizenship') and provided an admirably lucid and succinct description of the new paper's contents:

> The central idea in the paper is that young people should be enabled to develop capability for thoughtful and responsible participation in political, economic, social and cultural life. This is defined in terms of four aspects – knowledge and understanding, skills and competence, values and dispositions and creativity and enterprise. The paper also describes the types of opportunities and conditions for learning that schools and early years centres, working with parents and their communities, need to provide to facilitate progressive development. As well as focusing on implications for learning and teaching and for curriculum design, the paper emphasises two related core themes that need to be considered by schools, early years centres and local authorities.
>
> Firstly, young people learn most about citizenship by being active citizens. Schools should model the kind of society in which active citizenship is encouraged by providing all young people with opportunities to take on responsibilities and exercise choice. This requires the development of an open, participatory ethos, and management and organisation that recognises the importance of involving young people and everyone else with a stake in the learning community in the key decisions that affect them.
>
> Secondly, the development of capability for citizenship should be fostered in ways that motivate young people to be active and responsible members of their communities – local, national and global. Education for citizenship entails building bridges and developing interconnections between school or early years centre and community, to give young people opportunities to develop knowledge, understanding and care for the wider world.

It was never seriously considered in Scotland that there should be statutory reinforcement of the Executive's policies with regard to citizenship education. Of course this means in theory that schools would always be free to ignore what amounted only to advice from LTS and ministers. But LTS was fast acquiring the authority of an executive non-departmental public body which could easily voice ministerial views and policies, and in addition the Executive had HMIE (Her Majesty's Inspectorate of Education) to exert its powerful influence on the schools and colleges and education authorities. The inspectorate had been to some extent sidelined from policy making, but they were still routinely called upon to advise ministers and in their frequent inspections – not only of schools and colleges but also now of education authorities – they could monitor and assess the extent to which the staff were implementing the intentions of the authorities and attaining the learning outcomes specified for them in official statements and reports. GCF trustees were well aware of their influence and their potential for advancing the Foundation's purposes, and consequently I made arrangements to discuss a jointly funded project designed to bring citizenship education to the forefront in the inspection process. With funding from the GCF, the HMI Audit Unit, headed by Frank Crawford, seconded an Education Authority Adviser, Alex Gilchrist, to develop a document using performance indicators (PIs) to help schools to evaluate what they were doing in respect of citizenship education. This project fitted neatly into the inspectorate's powerful framework for school self-evaluation, 'How Good is Our School?': it offered teachers a range of indicators as to how they should deal with education for citizenship in the classrooms, in the school life generally and in the school's relations with the community. Given that LTS was simultaneously providing materials and staff development guidance, schools in Scotland were well supported in the complex tasks of catering for citizenship education. The youth education sector was well provided with guidance and exemplary materials by the central agency, Community Learning Scotland, whose staff had undertaken, with GCF funding, a wide-ranging and highly effective development project on 'Active Citizenship'.

In Wales, education for citizenship has to be understood in the context of the 'Curriculum Cymreig', which is concerned with the 'Welshness' of what is taught to young people in the schools in Wales. In the GCF Four Nations Conference held in London in May 2000 the Welsh briefing paper pointed out that 'since citizenship is an ideologically contested concept it was felt that community understanding embraced citizenship in a way that citizenship did not embrace community'. Citizenship education in Wales is officially included within the framework for Personal and Social Education (PSE). There is therefore no statutory underpinning of citizenship education as such. PSE was given statutory status in the autumn of 2003, and the Welsh Assembly Government issued a circular to that effect. The PSE framework details delivery around ten aspects: social, community, physical, sexual, emotional, spiritual, moral, vocational, learning and environmental. An All Wales PSE Network Group, set up in December 2003, is disseminating good practice in PSE, making links between the formal and informal sectors, and working with the Welsh Assembly Government (WAG) on the development of a strategy for the subject. The framework has a 'community aspect' which aims at encouraging pupils to be active citizens in local contexts, and this is intended to lead to their taking part in the life of the national community and in the global community. Political literacy has not been accorded a special place, but political education, particularly education in democracy, is recognised as integral. Attention to Welsh elements of citizenship education – methods of election and the roles of representatives at different levels, and the rights and responsibilities of citizens of Wales – is naturally important. The Assembly is currently promoting education for citizenship in a number of ways: a Working Group on Global Citizenship has been set up, and a guide on *Education for Sustainable Development and Global Citizenship* has been published by ACCAC (*Awdurdod Cymwysterau Cwricwlwm Ac Asesu Cymru* – Qualifications, Curriculum and Assessment Authority for Wales). Citizenship education is also advocated in a good-practice video, a visitor centre at the Assembly at the Pierhead, the setting up of school and student councils, local forums and Funky Dragon – the Children and Young People's Assembly for Wales. There is a perception in England that the absence of a dedicated subject called 'citizenship education' will make it difficult for Welsh schools to give the subject sufficient status and impact, but there seems no good reason why that should not be achieved within the governing curriculum of PSE, particularly when schools have PSE Coordinators and arrangements whereby each cross-curricular theme is the responsibility of an appropriately qualified member of staff. The new Welsh Baccalaureate which is currently being piloted will provide for assessment and practical activities in PSE.

The central advisory body in Northern Ireland, the Council for the Curriculum, Examinations and Assessment (CCEA), has been active for several years in the development of education for citizenship, mostly within the framework of cross-curricular themes, prominent among which is Education for Mutual Understanding (EMU). Resource materials are provided for a range of courses and modules such as 'Law in our Lives', and newly created bodies such as the Human Rights Commission and an Equality Commission provide opportunities for the CCEA to work with them. Carmel Gallagher, Development Manager 4–14, CCEA, told the 2002 Four Nations Conference about a Nine-point Programme of development which includes teacher training support, work on evaluation, cross-sectoral work, the writing of a shared 'Common Commitment' (similar to a manifesto), the fostering of links between citizenship education and religious education, developing links with the Human Rights Commission, further e-learning links, and the development of more opportunities for accreditation through different award schemes. The GCF's association with educators in Northern Ireland began with our sponsorship in 1996 of the Values Education Project and has continued to the present day; this has been one of the most fruitful of our projects, not only because it has contributed to the development of citizenship education in various forms but also because GCF trustees and our Scottish associates have learned much from our Northern Irish colleagues about the nature of their problems and the many solutions they have explored.

Coinciding with the GCF-sponsored Four Nations Conference of 2003, hosted by our Northern Ireland colleagues in Belfast, comprehensive resource packs were launched; these provide guidance and exemplifications for teaching such themes as 'Diversity and Inclusion', 'Equality and Social Justice', 'Democracy and Active Participation', 'Human Rights and Social Responsibility'. 'Pathways', the CCEA's folder which sets out for teachers the minimum statutory proposals for all learning areas and subject strands in Key Stage 3 (ages 11 to 14), describes the 'contributory strand', 'Local and Global Citizenship', in terms which would stand as representative of the best thinking about the subject in the world:

Local and Global Citizenship aims to develop the capacity of young people to participate positively and effectively in society, to influence democratic processes, and to make informed and responsible decisions as local and global citizens throughout their lives. Through looking at real-life situations and scenarios, pupils are provided with opportunities to explore and express their own values and attitudes about cultural, political, economic, personal and social issues in contemporary society and challenged to develop an appreciation of the needs and perspectives of others. Through developing skills of critical evaluation, informed decision making and responsible action, the aim is to help young people develop a morally and ethically sound value system based on internationally recognised principles of equality, human rights, justice and democracy. Teachers may help young people to see the relevance of citizenship to life now and in the future, by exploring fundamental questions, such as:

- What are the main influences that shape people's behaviour today?
- What rights and responsibilities do people have?
- Why are there so many conflicts over rights?
- What does it mean to exercise your rights responsibly?
- Why do we have laws and how?
- How can I make a difference?
- How can I use the skills and knowledge I have developed in this area in my future life and work?

This superlative work, the result of years of study, discussion, consultation and research by an expert team led by Carmel Gallagher, Bernie Kells, Alastair Walker and associates from all over the UK and the Republic of Ireland, has been handsomely offered freely to be shared by other workers in the field of citizenship education. An important asset for the team has been the collegial guidance and practical support of Professor Alan Smith, of the University of Ulster, and his colleagues.

The Four Nations Conferences have fulfilled a genuine need in the development of citizenship education throughout the UK. They have brought educators from the four nations together when there were no other opportunities for them to meet and discuss the many-faceted problems that confront them. Each year a hundred educators have been able to live together for a few days in comfortable surroundings and learn from each other, exchange information and materials, and plan together how to coordinate their efforts in the field. Together they have been able to consolidate their thinking about this complex subject, to refine their theoretical and practical knowledge and to reach a deeper understanding of its philosophical implications. It has been remarkable how much the participants have in common, despite the great variety of the systems they work in and the multiplicity of their problems. The collegial links achieved have been continued and enhanced by electronic communications and the exchange of papers and invitations to meetings. It is true to say that the GCF, with our colleagues in the IGE (Institute for Global Ethics) and the Citizenship Foundation and the CSV (Community Service Volunteers) – who have given us the leadership and professional expertise we could not ourselves provide – can claim that the Four Nations Conferences have truly made a difference. Arrangements are in hand to create a permanent organisation which will enable continuous collaboration.

Despite the enthusiasm of many teachers and the wealth of supporting guidance and teaching materials available, it cannot be claimed that citizenship education has already found its proper place in the work of schools. Even in England and Northern Ireland, where the government units set up to further the provision are sending out excellent supportive resources and funding many staff development facilities, the picture is still somewhat discouraging. Inspectors are finding that over half the schools visited do not have satisfactory arrangements for the management of the subject; in only one in five schools is the curriculum well developed; the standards of knowledge and understanding among the pupils are poor. It is reported that the training of teachers is still patchy and that resources for community activities are insufficient. In England there are 'citizenship coordinators', who have been given special training, but too many of the teachers feel that they have not had satisfactory preparation for the subject's demands. Although the subject can be taken as an option in the GCSE (General Certificate in Secondary Education), it is still felt by many teachers that it lacks the power to motivate pupils that compulsory subjects have. Because it is still optional, the subject is often denied dedicated classroom time. Education Authorities are giving too little support. The greatest weakness appears to be that it is difficult to provide opportunities to join the pupils' learning to actual experience, for example in community involvement, democratic participation in school governance and so on. In other parts of the UK the situation is less clear but it can be assumed that schools are facing similar (probably greater) difficulty, especially because full subject status has not been achieved.

Citizenship education depends to a great extent on its ability to motivate and excite the pupils. Being a set of activities and experiences involving personal commitment and the acceptance of individual responsibility and willing teamwork, it cannot take for granted that pupils will give time and effort for their own future gratification in the form of exam passes or certificates. They need to apply themselves for immediate pleasure – for fun – with the added incentive of being able to take pride in achievement. That is the value of award schemes: some means of recognising individual or group achievement, by giving them something tangible to enjoy. One of the more picturesque results of one of the Windsor Castle consultations organised by Sheila Bloom of IGE UK has been an award scheme called *Impetus*. The occasion of its conception was a discussion of the Human Rights Act, which came into force in October 2000, and how young people can be taught about human rights and responsibilities. The government had set up a unit in the Home Office to work with educators and others on this problem, and at Windsor some of us seized upon the idea of creating a scheme of awards for schools and youth groups. Our thinking was bold and our plans large. We would seek sponsors to help us set up a national, UK-wide, programme of awards to 'recognise, reward and celebrate schools and youth organisations that have made a commitment to good practice in values-based approaches to education for citizenship or Personal and Social Education (PSE), in the context of the Human Rights Act'. Initial funding was given by the Home Office (and later the Lord Chancellor's Department, now the Department for Constitutional Affairs) and the GCF, as the major sponsors, with contributions from the DfES and the Comino Foundation. Sheila agreed to manage the project, and part-time staff were appointed in the four nations to act as coordinators. Because hundreds of schools and youth groups all over the UK were to be involved, a fairy elaborate structure of administrators and advisers was required: in time we set up a national Advisory Panel, local Voluntary Panels, regional coordinators and Country Panels. The central administration is a partnership between the IGE UK and the Citizenship Foundation. Now in its third year, *Impetus* is well established. There have been two national award ceremonies, many local celebrations and a large number of very enthusiastic and successful projects in many areas of the UK. The scheme is not yet universal, because funding has been difficult to sustain; but it is still growing, and it has generated immense enthusiasm among young people all over the UK. This is because the youngsters and their teachers find it attractive as a way of doing creative work to celebrate human rights, and gratifying to receive the recognition the scheme affords.

Chapter Sixteen

Education for character and moral competence

What Victor Cook meant by 'education for character' is evidenced by the dedicated themes of his Deed of Trust. Education for citizenship, in his mind, meant the transmission of the values and qualities that make a person a 'good citizen' possessing the virtues of honesty, compassion (care for others) and loyalty (respect for lawful authority), and the knowledge and commitment that make a person useful and competent in participating in the management of society's political life. Education for 'character' (he believed that the schools should be concerned with the *development* of character) was part and parcel of the same endeavour, to help young people to hold the values essential to being a good person. These values are both explicit and implicit in his own writings, in his use of quotations and in the materials he produced for schools. He was convinced that the values and the connected qualities of character need to be learned. His faithful attachment to the psychological notions which underpin William McDougall's model of human conduct reflected his intuitive conviction that human beings are on the whole born with instinctive dispositions towards living in peace and harmony. In McDougall's terms, these qualities express in human behaviour such instincts as gregariousness, self-defence mechanisms and the conduct necessary for the survival of the 'herd' – in modern parlance the community and the wider society. Like McDougall, Victor recognised the occurrence of aberrant behaviour and its extreme manifestations of cruelty and arrogance and tyranny; but he was unwilling to accept that bad conduct was not amenable to correction through education. He could not ignore large-scale evil as demonstrated by the Holocaust or the oppression of minorities in different parts of the world, but he wanted educators to concentrate on devising educational experiences with the potential of rectifying selfish behaviour and developing altruism: he advocated the study of role models for better ways of living, examining one's own conduct and seeking ways for improving it, the study of past political and social movements and the discussion of moral dilemmas in ordinary life. In short, he firmly believed that values education held answers to the sociomoral problems that confront 'good men and women', who constitute the great majority of humankind. In this Victor mirrored the moral persuasions of the majority of educated people in the world, the people who live lives of quiet industriousness, getting on with their ordinary affairs, intent on 'doing their duty' by their families and neighbours, hoping to do well without hurting anyone else – the doves, the sheep, the farmers of history, the 'decent folk'. That they are always in danger from the hawks, the wolves, the savage hunters who would invade their peace and exploit their innocence was not a recurrent anxiety for Victor; but he accepted that there were malign forces at work which threatened to destroy the peace and undermine the 'character' of the people. Like so many of his kind, he believed in a golden past where people were more virtuous. He subscribed without question to the apocalyptic fear of social disorder and moral decay so cogently voiced in the books and newspaper articles he read. But his whole life was dedicated to educational action designed to reverse the trend.

To Victor Cook the qualities of compassion and tolerance qualified by determination to 'do the right thing' and promote 'right thinking', what nowadays we would characterise as 'moral courage' – were essential to good citizenship. It was the prime task of the education system in a civilised country to produce the good citizens of tomorrow, and this was the governing motivation for his Foundation. He was often daunted by the enormity of his undertaking; he knew that all of his wealth would be needed even to make a beginning. In his modesty he thought that wealth was all that he had to offer, and he was always on the lookout for other sources of support, inviting wealthy acquaintances like Bertram Tawse to join his trustees and making approaches to other foundations like the Farmington Trust; sadly he usually met with polite indifference or unwillingness to match his own prescriptions. But he remained cautiously optimistic to his dying day. The importance to modern educators of people like Victor Cook is that they are essentially ordinary: they represent the majority of hardworking, materially comfortable people who form the backbone of the democratic societies of the world. Often narrow-minded and confused, frequently wrong, their judgements seldom the result of intensive reflection or genuine research, they are nevertheless much more like the huge majority of the young people we educate than are the bookish intellectuals who assume responsibility for interpreting the world of thought on their behalf.

Although the nurturing of 'good character' has figured in British educational policy documents for nearly two centuries, the term *character education* has been imported from the USA. The American Institute for

Character Education (with which Victor Cook associated himself) became influential during the presidencies of Reagan and the elder Bush: it called for the development of 'good character' through schooling, and variously described *character* as a combination of persistent qualities such as courage, generosity, kindness, honesty, tolerance, and a commitment to freedom of speech, human equality, independence and diligence. In more recent times the Character Education Partnership in the USA has swept all these qualities into its 'Eleven Principles of Effective Character Education'. In brief, these comprise:

1. The assertion of 'widely shared, pivotally important core ethical values' such as caring, honesty, fairness, responsibility and respect for self and others. Schools should stand for these values, define them, model them, study them and make all school members accountable to standards of conduct consistent with them.

2. Understanding the composite nature of 'good character': 'moral knowing' (knowing about moral values, being able to reason in moral terms, etc.); 'moral feeling' (loving the good, empathy, self-control, etc.); and 'moral action' (commitment to doing good things).

3. Promotion in schools of a proactive approach to developing character; using every possible opportunity throughout all aspects of school life and work to contribute to character development.

4. Embodying the values in the whole school community: imbuing all activities with core values.

5. Giving students 'repeated moral experiences': involving them in cooperative learning, community improvement projects, conflict resolution, etc.

6. Ensuring that the curriculum promotes character development: using student-centred, active learning, problem-solving approaches, etc.

7. Developing intrinsic motivation: fostering respect for learning; minimising reliance on extrinsic rewards and punishment; encouraging collaborative learning, etc.

8. Developing the whole staff as a moral community: all must model the core values in their own behaviour; involving all staff in developmental activities; involving all staff in discussion of moral matters and participating in character-developing experiences for students.

9. Championship of character education by leaders such as principals, senior management, governors and other influential persons.

10. Recruiting parents and other members of the community as full partners in the character-building efforts.

11. Evaluation of every aspect of the enterprise: assessing progress in character development; assessing the school staff's growth as character educators; surveying students' understanding of and commitment to action on the core values; assessing students' moral knowledge and judgement, their moral commitment, and their moral behaviour.

These principles and applications have been adopted widely in the USA, where there is strong federal and state support for practical development programmes. Allowing for differences in terminology we can discern very similar statements of principle in many official and staff development publications in the UK and other European education systems. There is, however, one outstanding and crucial difference. In almost all our policy documents there is little or no commitment to proactive, system-wide action. Moral education is universally agreed to be a prime responsibility of the school, but it is never given – in any form or under any set of terms – a prominent role as a school function. It is generally assumed that – apart from its inclusion with religious education – moral education inhabits every activity as a kind of ghost, without actual physical presence. In the USA – in the states, that is, that have adopted specific policies for moral education programmes – teachers have the assurance that the authorities require them to teach in accordance with the guidance issued to them. In the UK, teachers only have nebulous advice accorded them; even in England, with its statutory requirements for citizenship education, broader moral education is still stipulated as an adjunct to religious education and personal and health education. Old outmoded presumptions of earlier twentieth-century policies seem still to prevail – that there can be no such thing as moral education outside the Religious Education classroom, and in any case we do not know how to teach it. These are no longer valid objections: in recent years moral education – usually with the label of values education – has been accorded wide recognition and has been the subject of a large body of experimental development work. It is clearly evident in this book that in each of the constituent nations of the UK there is a strong thrust towards the teaching of values and applicative experiential activities. The advent of citizenship education has opened up the whole field: in Scotland, for example, the relevant 'national priority' is called 'values and citizenship'; in Wales, the national priority is called 'personal and social education'; and in Northern Ireland the new curricular guidelines encompass all the characteristics described in the USA for character education.

Conscious of the need to provide teachers and their managers with specific models of a successful values education system, the GCF decided to send a team of educators to see and evaluate the values-driven system in Maine. Here the enlightened Commissioner for Education, Duke Albanese, with the support of the Governor, Angus King, had set up a Commission for Ethical and Responsible Student Behavior to draft standards that would guide school districts across the state. They were fortunate that Camden, Maine, was the headquarters of the Institute for Global Ethics (IGE), already famous for its pioneering work on introducing principles and practices in ethical training to businesses, public service organisations, schools and colleges and communities. Its founder and leading inspiration, Rushworth Kidder, author of such seminal works as *Shared Values for a Troubled World*, *Moral Courage* and *How Good People Make Tough Choices* was invited to co-chair the Commission, and its report, *Taking Responsibility* (2001), set out a coherent rationale for the adoption of ethical standards throughout the education system, a theoretical framework for moral education and a set of 'hallmarks' of an ethical and responsible school culture. These hallmarks comprise the establishment of collectively identified core values, community participation in the process of value clarification, the involvement of students in all the activities, active partnership with parents, the integration of values education in the whole curriculum and culture of the school (not to be viewed as an 'extra'), an interventionist and inclusive disciplinary process which is 'impartial, consistent and educational', and the careful definition and assessment of outcomes. For each hallmark the report sets out 'sample strategies' for the actual educational expression of the core values, which it suggests might be Respect, Honesty, Compassion, Fairness, Responsibility and Courage.

The purpose of our visit to Maine was threefold. I had been impressed by the methodology constructed by the IGE for initiating people into the processes of discussing moral questions, identifying and defining moral values, consensus building to reach a pragmatic rank-ordering of important values, and using this framework in the action of producing coherent, if tentative, answers to moral dilemmas drawn from everyday life; and firstly I wanted a group of educators, highly experienced and expert in their own field but not familiar with moral educational procedures, to undergo some training in the techniques. Secondly, in discussing the project with Sheila Bloom, chief executive of the UK affiliate of IGE, I wanted the team to visit schools, see their versions of values education in action, and evaluate them in the light of the question, 'What, if anything, should we carry home to adapt and apply in Scotland?'

Thirdly, I hoped the team might form a small *corps d'elite* of innovators working together to transform the prevailing cultures in Scottish education. We chose a team from Scotland because the system was comparatively small and well integrated, the team members shared a common outlook and background as educators, and we felt that further action at home could be taken easily and our findings shared later with colleagues in England, Wales and Northern Ireland. We hoped the team would be representative of the various sections of Scottish education; but the governing consideration was that they would be powerful – intellectually and in terms of their personal influence. In the event we were outstandingly fortunate. The team comprised individuals of high intellectual quality, great practical experience and a sensible taste for innovation. Stewart Jardine was a consultant doing a variety of jobs for the Scottish Executive and local education authorities; in his background was experience as a secondary head teacher and a chief regional adviser, and a depth of knowledge about educational assessment and school improvement. Anne Macintosh was an authority on religious education, a former education development officer in an education authority and now a development officer with Learning and Teaching Scotland (LTS). Gordon Jeyes was Director of Children's Services in Stirling and a leading figure in the Association of Directors of Education in Scotland (ADES). Mike McCabe was also a Director of Education – in South Ayrshire – and an energetic and innovative educational manager. Mary McLaughlin was head of an important girls' school, Notre Dame High School, and a highly experienced educator as well as a popular member of a number of official planning bodies. Frank Lennon was one of the country's leading head teachers: his school, St Modan's High School, was famed for its high quality in scholastic achievement and also in its development of character. Judith Sischy, Chief Executive of the Scottish Council for Independent Schools, was an outstanding educational manager and a shrewd and imaginative educator. Professor Tom Wilson was Principal of Glasgow College of Building and Printing, a professor at the Caledonian University and chair of a number of public bodies, including LTS. With Sheila Bloom of IGE (UK) and her colleagues in IGE (US) to support us, we enjoyed the best possible opportunity to see an education system of high quality, and schools which were outstandingly successful in imbuing all their work and social activities with values selected and defined by the students, staff and community supporters. We returned home to Scotland determined to lead a culture change which would inspire the system and enable all its parts to achieve new greatness in quality and practical effectiveness. Subsequently we have met as a group, working hard to express our ideas in forms which would help our various colleagues to appreciate their roles with a fresh realisation of their mission as educators. We were aware that Scottish education had always been strongly imbued with values: we were not offering revolutionary notions, but rather encouraging the building of a coherent culture deriving from agreed core values. The presentation we put together, under the leadership of Mike McCabe, begins with the values engraved on the mace of the renewed parliament of Scotland: Compassion, Wisdom, Justice, Integrity; and we set out to persuade our political leaders to reaffirm their faith in these values and encourage every organisation under their authority to embark upon the process of analysing, clarifying and codifying their professional and personal values. We suggested that the national priorities identified by the Executive should be elaborated in terms of values, and that these values should be used to stimulate the life and work of all schools and institutions. Because the values that underpin the national priorities have never been subjected to this kind of analysis, there is a lack of clarity in the public understanding of what the education system is setting out to do for the young. A values-based approach will throw stronger light on the many initiatives we are putting into operation. It would address various issues such as 'ownership', understanding and balance: it would improve people's understanding of the 'prioritised agenda' and deepen our pupils' awareness of their roles as citizens in the new millennium. A values-based approach to schooling in all its aspects would give education for citizenship a firmer foundation. It would provide:

- a shared strategic vision, understood and committed to by all;
- a basis for selecting, sequencing and planning new initiatives;
- a mechanism for managing potential tensions arising between different national priorities; and
- a strategic framework for developing and refining the national priorities.

The operational benefits of a values-based approach are clear to anyone who has become familiar with the rationale – as were those of us who saw the system developed in the state of Maine. It would transform staff attitudes, principally by moving from a model of compliance – doing what you are told, leaving it to your superiors to pronounce upon the reasons why you should meet the requirements of the authorities and so on – to a model of commitment: believing in what you do, understanding why we do things as we do, above all having a sense of 'ownership' because you have been personally involved in constructing the rationale which underpins your work. Individuals and teams are encouraged to contribute to the development of the rationale, so that they are all familiar with and committed to the policies and practices which emerge over time. A values-based approach provides what we have called 'a strategic compass' which enables individual members of staff – or teams, such as school staffs or education authorities' management – to step back from the detailed implementation of policies and maintain a 'sense of direction' as to where the policies will lead the organisation. It helps to marry 'local ownership' with nationally identified policies, preventing these from becoming a mere list of dislocated requirements. Our 'big idea', then, is to help the education system to become 'values driven' at all levels. Core values would permeate professional thinking and working, serving as reference points as people plan new developments and work out how they might best be implemented.

The development of these ideas can usefully begin with 'seminars' at which groups of people – from any part of an organisation – are taken through the processes designed by the IGE. The seminar begins with a general introduction to the language of values discussion: what do we mean by 'values'? – what values do we recognise at work in our society and in our personal lives? – out of a fairly random list of values suggested by participants, which would we agree to be 'core' values? By this process it is possible to refine one's perception of the meaning of the terms we bandy about: for example, *compassion* might emerge as a kind of portmanteau term containing such concepts as *caring, consideration, charity*, and so on. Participants are led through the IGE's Ethical Fitness™ training programme; this has been methodically developed through many years and is formally trademarked. In the course of a seminar (of one day or longer) the participants experience a study of 'moral awareness' (how to define 'ethics' in terms of people's responses to social situations); how to define values and, in particular, ethical values; how to analyse morally ambivalent situations in terms of 'dilemma paradigms' such as 'truth versus loyalty', 'self versus community', 'short-term versus long-term', 'justice versus mercy'. IGE staff are experts in guiding ordinary persons through these processes, in the course of which they are given constructive insights into the different ways moral philosophers – both past and present – resolve the complex questions relating to moral conduct in ordinary life and in the social and political movements which preoccupy the modern world. We would like to see planners and decision makers undergoing these experiences, so that they can apply the wisdom to their own work and help to develop a values-imbued education system for schools and other institutions.

We are, of course, well aware of the difficulties. Values are themselves difficult concepts, and the questions that arise about education in values – or ethical or moral education of any brand – are naturally complex and problematical. The expositions and methodologies being proposed are unavoidably simplistic; but then all teaching requires simplification to some extent – the need is to be assured that it is effective without losing validity. That assurance can only come from painstaking applied research and experimentation: ultimately it is only when practitioners have studied the rationale, trialled the variety of approaches being proffered, and evaluated their validity and practical administrability and arrived at wholehearted endorsement of them that direct moral teaching in acceptable forms can be achieved.

Victor Cook's vision is already being given practical form in modern education. All the teaching methods being developed for 'values and citizenship' in the different parts of the UK encompass methods for developing 'moral and social awareness', but there remains the need for methods to be developed for teaching 'moral reasoning' – the ability to arrive rationally at a valid interpretation of a moral issue, and the ability to justify logically the conclusion arrived at for application in real life. Since moral values are independent, usually, of their source, moral teaching of this kind can be conducted outside or within the teaching of religious education: there seems to be no reason, as Cook often asserted, why values education should conflict in any serious way with religious education. Thus under the banner of *values and citizenship* we can achieve all that Victor Cook dreamed of: the school, in partnership with parents and members of the community it serves, can help our young people to grow up as caring and responsible citizens, committed to supporting what is good and productive in the estimation of themselves and their mentors, able to identify what is right and what is wrong, and able and willing to do whatever lies in their power to make the world a better place.

Notes and references

1. The life and times of Victor Cook

1. I owe the account of Victor Cook's career largely to a paper by Dr Peter Clarke, *Robert Charles Victor Cook*, now in the Foundation archives at 3 Chattan Place, Aberdeen, AB10 6RB.
2. The quotation from Carlyle is from his essay, *Past and Present*, 1843.
3. Victor was 17 when the Second World War broke out. We have no knowledge of his attitude towards joining up, as tens of thousands of boys of his age did; presumably he left school at 18 and went on to study engineering – and perhaps worked in the family engineering works part-time – both of which occupations would have been regarded as 'reserved'.

2. Towards the Foundation

1. William McDougall's book, *Character and the Conduct of Life*, was published by Methuen in 1927. The version Victor used was a third edition, published in 1928. He bought it second-hand at some time after 1931 – it had been a prize given to a pupil of Oulton School, Liverpool. Victor's scorings and marginal notes indicate passages that particularly impressed him.
2. E. B. Castle's books *Moral Education in Christian Times* (1958) and *The Teacher* (Oxford University Press, 1970) were popular reading for student teachers. In the 1980s, when the latter book was out of print, Victor had sections of it reproduced for use by students and teachers.

3. Victor as lobbyist

1. Cook was almost wholly ignorant of the practical problems facing Scottish educational managers in the sixties and seventies. These are described and discussed in *Governing Education* by Andrew McPherson and Charles D. Raab (Edinburgh University Press, 1988).
2. Nearly all the information about Cook's activities as described in this chapter is derived from his own notes and correspondence preserved in the GCF archives. His correspondence with Education Department officials was disposed of many years ago.

4. The Plan and the Deed

1. All the documents quoted here are from files kept by Victor himself.

2. It is worth remembering that Victor's grant of £100,000 in 1974 was the equivalent of more than ten times that amount in present-day terms.

5. Political constraints

1. The political and educational context against which Cook's efforts should be read are described, for Scotland, in Gatherer, W. A., *Curriculum Development in Scotland* (Scottish Academic Press, 1989) and in MacBeath, John, *Personal and Social Education* (Scottish Academic Press, 1988); and, for England and Wales, in *Handbook of Educational Ideas and Practices*, ed. Noel Entwistle (Routledge, 1990).

6. Developments in moral education: theory and practice

1. The impact of the Plowden Report and the Scottish Primary Memorandum can be best understood from John Darling's *Child-centred Education and its Critics* (Paul Chapman, 1994).
2. For contemporary perspectives on moral education, see papers by John White and Glynn Phillips in *Handbook of Educational Ideas and Practices* (Routledge, 1990). My own paper on *The Teaching of Literature* in the same volume rejects the notion of literature as moral teaching.
3. The significance of the Munn Report and other publications of the Consultative Committee on the Curriculum can be understood from various accounts in *Scottish Education*, ed. T. G. K. Bryce and W. M. Humes (Edinburgh University Press, 2003).

7. The failure of the pedagogy

1. The critical analyses of the materials issued by the Cook team were printed internally in the Northern College, Aberdeen, and are in the GCF archives.

8. The way towards public acceptance

1. The report on 'Responsibility Education' is in the GCF archives. The papers by Alex Sharp and George Thomson were published by the University of Indiana in *Viewpoints in Teaching and Learning*, 1981.
2. Lickona's work, *Educating for Character* (Bantam, 1992) is a seminal book of guidance to classroom activities in values education.

9. The 1980s: progress

1. The kits, log books and so on distributed by the Cook team are only of 'historical' value; samples have been kept in the GCF archives.
2. The reports cited in this chapter are discussed variously in *Scottish Education* (Edinburgh University Press, 2003).
3. The political issues of the period are described in depth in McPherson and Raab, *Governing Education* (Edinburgh University Press, 1988), and in lesser

detail in Bryce and Humes, *Scottish Education* (Edinburgh University Press, 2003).

4. The history of the strike of 1984–6 and its aftermath is given in Willis Pickard's paper, 'The History of Scottish Education 1980 to the present day' in Bryce and Humes, ibid.

5. The importance of Bart McGettrick's acquisition as a trustee cannot be exaggerated. He was then and has continued to be a distinguished and influential member of the Scottish establishment. As Principal of St Andrew's College, and later Dean of the Education Faculty of Glasgow University, and as a lecturer and writer, he is an outstanding educationist; he has been a member of many important committees and advisory groups, Vice Chairman of the SCCC and chairman of several official study groups, author of many papers on curriculum and values. He has been honoured with the OBE and several honorary doctorates. In the Catholic Church he is Knight Commander with Star of the Holy Sepulchre of Jerusalem and holder of the Silver Palm of Jerusalem. He has contributed valuably to the prestige and influence of the GCF, not least because his presence on the Board of Trustees testifies to the easy relationship between our campaign for values education and religious education.

6. Henry Drummond (1851–97) was Professor of Natural Science at the free Church College in Glasgow. His book *Natural Law in the Spiritual World* (1883), an attempt to reconcile Christian beliefs to the theory of evolution, was immensely popular in his time. His book *The Greatest Thing in the World* was circulated in cheap editions throughout the lifetime of Victor's mother; the 'greatest thing' was, of course, Christianity.

10. Triumphs and anxieties

1. The accession to the post of secretary to the Foundation of David Levie, senior partner of Burnett and Reid, our lawyers, was a distinct advantage: he learned much about our work and committed himself to our purposes; and he produced formal minutes, which had not been done before.

2. Michael Forsyth was an active but controversial minister. One of the Tory 'no turning back' Group, he was determined to introduce the right-wing policies proposed in the Black Papers of the mid-seventies.

3. The events recorded here relating to the GCF's approach to the SCCC have not been written up before. I owe the information to papers kept by Victor and personal recollections.

4. W. D. Wall was an educational psychologist; he had been head of UNESCO's Education and Child Development Unit, Director of NFER, and Professor of Educational Psychology at the University of London Institute of Education. His book *The Adolescent Child* (Methuen, 1948, 1952, 1956) was widely read in teacher training.

5. Victor's acceptance that the proposed Centre should be set up as an official

agency was due to the persuasions of his trustees; but his decision to fund the Centre separately from the Foundation's funds was due to his determination to carry on with his 'own' work, which might have been set aside by an official centre.

6. The Agreement drafted by David McNicoll went through several versions because Victor insisted on the inclusion of clauses which the officers considered to be too prescriptive. Victor was frequently adjured that he must 'go with the grain' of official policy but he was never happy to do so.

11. Tributes

1. Victor Cook's will and the Deed of Trust are in the keeping of the Foundation and its lawyers.

2. The reports and supporting papers resulting from the research and development projects mentioned here are in the keeping of the institutions. It was our normal practice to initiate a scheme, appoint directors, and provide funds; thereafter we preferred the organisations themselves to publish their findings, and we were comfortable that they should benefit from any revenues. An important project which emerged at this time was ROVE (Research on Values Education), directed by Eileen Francis of Moray House. This was a study of how a values education programme might be developed for students aged 14-plus. Eileen arranged a multifaceted programme of consultations, seminars and experimental courses which aroused interest among a very wide range of students and teachers. Long after her initial project was completed, she continued to involve people in her programme of research, discussion and reports – under the title VECTOR, which indicated 'values education', 'consultation' and 'research' – which came to be established as a powerful networking of interested and committed people from different walks of life. VECTOR was, and is, an achievement which merits a book to itself and it is to be hoped that one may one day record her achievements.

3. Professor Haldane set the themes after discussion with trustees, invited speakers, arranged for venues and edited the papers for publication. It is pleasing to note that the texts are to be published again shortly.

4. The papers by Neville Stewart, Bill Horton and Jeff Bagnall were written for the trustees and are in the GCF archives.

12. Towards a theory of values education

1. In the USA and in the Republic of South Africa, strenuous efforts are made to make the values underpinning the work of government explicit and acknowledged throughout the systems. This is not the case in the UK. While values essential to democratic governance are frequently expressed in official documents, structures of government are not 'values driven' in the sense that staff are informed of and required to apply the values overtly in their work. A new movement, partly inspired by the Four Nations Conferences (see Chapter 15),

is in action to persuade politicians and their executives to adopt values-driven procedures.

2. David Carr's important book *Educating the Virtues* (Routledge, 1991) on the philosophical and psychological bases of moral development and education has been influential in professional philosophy and educational theory, but it seems too difficult for ordinary educators to access and use in their everyday activity. He has, however, written and delivered many papers which enable educators to reach a deeper understanding of the subject.

3. The SCCC's position on values education changed perceptibly with the retiral of David McNicoll and his senior officers, Keith Robinson and Sydney Smyth. Partly because of new pressures from government to give greater priority to targets and standards in the core subjects, and partly because of a sharper scepticism among new staff, the SCCC swerved away from the clarity and commitment of the early nineties. Under the leadership of Ian Barr and Margaret McGhie, however, some thoughtful papers were issued which endorsed the importance of thinking about values.

13. The campaign in the nineties

1. The controversies aroused by Michael Forsyth's policies are dealt with in detail in *Curriculum and Assessment in Scotland*, ed. Angela Roger and David Hartley (Scottish Academic Press, 1990).

2. During the comparatively short period during which Bill Robb was chief executive he accomplished much useful work. His departure was the result of difficulties about his role in relation to the chairman. After that event the everyday business of the Foundation was managed by the chairman and the secretary.

3. The papers issued by the SCCC during this period are now in the library of its successor, Learning and Teaching Scotland (LTS).

4. The report of the project on 'Values in the Nursery School' was published by the University of Paisley.

5. Bridge Somekh's evaluation report is in the archives of the GCF. The trustees studied her recommendations carefully and implemented many of them. We have failed, however, to adopt her proposals about the appointment of new trustees.

6. The project we initiated in Northern Ireland in 1996 reached a triumphant consummation in 2003. At the Four Nations conference in Belfast, the work of Alison Montgomery and her team was launched in the form of a handsomely designed package of teaching materials.

7. The period of Marvin Berkowitz's work in Scotland had a major influence on his own career and consequently on the development of moral education internationally. He has developed the 'moral anatomy' first explicated in his monograph, *The Education of the Complete Moral Person*, published by the GCF in 1996. He is now Professor of Character Education at the University of

Missouri-St Louis, and founder and co-editor of a new journal on Character Education.

8. The reports of the GCF Conferences in 1995, 1996, 1997, 1998 and 1999 were published by the institutions which collaborated with the Foundation in mounting them; copies are lodged in the GCF library. Information is available on the website we commissioned from the University of Bristol: http://www.becal.net. This is being developed by Dr Ruth Deakin Crick and her colleagues at the Graduate School of Bristol University. In cooperation with Bart McGettrick, Ruth is providing updated information on a wide range of GCF projects, bringing our work into the sphere of moral education world-wide.

14. New emphases: values education for health and enterprise

1. The 'Police Box' remains the property of the Grampian Police Service. Most of the police services in the UK have purchased a box, and the materials are being adapted and extended in many schools.

2. The report *An Education for Life and Work* was issued by the then government department for education.

3. *Values Compared* was issued informally. A copy may be obtained from the GCF.

4. *FACE (Facilitated Assessment for Chief Executives)* was published, with GCF support, by Quality Scotland.

5. The report of the 1996 conference, *Changing Contexts for Values Education*, was published by the GCF in partnership with St Andrew's College (now incorporated in Glasgow University). (ISBN 1 898220 23 9).

6. *Determined to Succeed* was issued by the Scottish Executive.

7. Another produce of our desire to influence people engaged in the world of work was the Gordon Cook Conversations. Held in congenial surroundings, these events engage persons of the 35 to 45 age range in discussions about their values and how they would wish to see society developing over the next decade. The organiser for the GCF is John Moorhouse, whose experience in industry and business, and his work in innovative public education enterprises, has equipped him to make the experience highly productive as well as enjoyable for the participants.

8. The Gordon Cook Conversations introduced us to Gavin Ross, who is now a trustee of GCF and our current chairman. Experienced both as a practitioner and a lecturer in Architecture, Gavin has also achieved distinction as a manager of higher education, having been Principal of Edinburgh College of Art and Vice Principal of Robert Gordon University. Gavin's reasons for accepting our invitation to become a trustee are worth recording here because they throw fresh light on the social and educational mission the Foundation has gradually developed over many years:

When I graduated as an architect and town planner in the mid-sixties it was my intention to work in the public sector. I wanted to do work that related to society as a whole and also to embrace in a wide sense the whole question of designing and creating the world around us as experienced by all members of society. In particular I was interested in the place of living within the scheme of things and how that should relate to all our other activities. . . . I wanted to play my part in building for society as a whole . . . to use the skills of an architect to better the built world that society inhabits . . . Had it not been for the withdrawal of belief in the public sector in the late seventies and the subsequent disbanding of the great public architectural offices, I would have made my career in that sector. Looking back I suppose I was old enough to realise what a near squeak we had had with the Second World War, and I relished the challenge to put my abilities to use in the rebuilding of our towns and cities so as to best serve the new society that had emerged as a result of the consequences of that time.

I have also had a committed belief in the notion of the teacher practitioner: indeed I feel it is the duty of the practitioner to teach, so I was not only trying to build a career as an architect and town planner but I was also working at developing a capability as a teacher of those subjects. After all teaching is the best way to learn, and one's students nourish one's thinking to an extent not nearly so readily attained working on one's own. I also believed completely in the personal value to the student of fostering learning. Not least because I felt the complexities and dilemmas of co-existing in the company of one's fellow citizens in a crowded and highly developed and demanding environment typical of late twentieth century towns and cities present all of us with issues and decisions as to how to conduct our lives. In short, to have civilised cities one must have civilised citizens . . . You can see therefore how the objectives of the Gordon Cook Foundation would resonate with longstanding interests that I have in the making of towns and cities.

15. Education for citizenship

1. Materials used by the Centre for Citizenship Studies in Education are available from the centre, now housed in the University of Leicester.
2. The report of the GCF conference of 1991 is in the GCF archives.
3. Jerome Bruner's seminal thinking on learning is set out in his book *Towards a Theory of Instruction* (Harvard University Press, 1967). In subsequent years, particularly during his period of work at Oxford, Bruner worked closely with Scottish educators at the Scottish Council for Research in Education (SCRE).
4. The statement referred to is in the *Subject Guide, Modern Studies* published by SCCC in 1997.
5. See Warden, D. A. and Christie, D. F. M., *Teaching Social Behaviour* (David Fulton, 1997): this is a set of resources designed to promote 'interpersonal awareness, the understanding of relationships and prosocial behaviour'.

6. There is an account of the development of LTS (from the SCCC) in George MacBride's chapter in *Scottish Education*, ed. Bryce and Humes (Edinburgh University Press, 2003).

7. 'Curriculum Cymreig' and its significance for citizenship education are described in papers by Rhys Andrews and Gari Lewis (*Citizenship Education in Wales: Community, Culture and the Curriculum Cymreig*, NFER, 2001) and Rhys Andrews (*Policy Development for Citizenship Education in Wales*, NFER, 2001).

8. CCEA has published an information pack, *Pathways*, setting out the curriculum for young people in Northern Ireland aged 11–14. In the section 'Learning for Life and Work' the concepts, learning outcomes and teaching approaches for 'Local and Global Citizenship' are expertly presented.

9. As the disseminated guidance for *Impetus* makes clear, the scheme seeks to promote values such as mutual respect, honesty and integrity, fairness of treatment, personal freedom and personal responsibility. These materials can be obtained from the Institute for Global Ethics, UK Trust, 3–4 Bentinck Street, London, W1U 2EE.

16. Education for character and moral competence

1. Victor Cook never voiced personal opinions about the political movements of our time. He was, however, an enthusiast for the teaching of World Studies and the discussion of different points of view.

2. Cook's conservative belief in a 'golden past' and the moral defection of contemporary society was reflected in the quotations he used in his writings. He did not, however, subscribe to any form of extremist ideology.

3. Information about 'character education' is available from the Character Education Partnership (CEP) based in Washington DC, USA (http://www.character.org).

4. Rushworth Kidder's *How Good People Make Tough Choices* is published by Simon and Schuster NY, 1996. Other works by Rushworth M. Kidder may be obtained from the Institute for Global Ethics, Cambden, Maine, USA.

Index

References to notes are indicated by page(chapter.note), e.g. 171(10.4)